CLPE
Centre for Language in Primary Education
(London Borough of Southwark)
Webber Row
London SE1 8QW

Thanks to the following members of CLPE staff for their help in the production of this book
Doris Anstee
Brenda Hockley
and to Norris Bentham for her work on the manuscript.

Design: Maddison/Moore Graphics
Photography: Phil Polglaze, Shades
Printed by: Marstan Press
Typeface: Cheltenham, Frutiger

© Centre for Language in Primary Education

First published in 1991 by CLPE

ISBN 1-872267-03-3

Printed and bound in the U.K.

Contents

Acknowledgements

The Reading Book began as a CLPE working party on reading which met for over a year in 1988/90 and discussed what would need to be included in a teachers' guide to reading. Papers by the working party resulted in an original manuscript which contributed substantially to the thinking behind the present book. We would like to thank all the members of this working party, whose names are listed below, and are particularly grateful to Alison Kelly and Sue Smedley for their work on the original manuscript, and to Healther Mines for her draft of the original introduction.

Bunmi Akala	Heather Mines
Penny Bentley	Jane Preest
Manjula Datta	Ian Russell
Karen Feeney	Vicki Ryle
Maggie Futcher	Sue Smedley
Alison Kelly	Jill Verde
Patience MacGregor	Sally Yates
Beverley Mackenzie	Staff of CLPE

We thank Bannockburn School for allowing us to reproduce their reading policy in its entirety as the Appendix to this book.
We thank Jill Verde and Margaret Wyeth for the interviews in *Teachers talking about teaching*.
We thank Alison Kelly and Alyson Russen for their contributions to *A day in the life of a reader*.
We thank Leila O'Sullivan for the illustration to *Reading Media*

We thank the following schools, which have given their permission to use examples of their work in this book:
Bannockburn Primary School
Columbia Primary School
Conway Junior School
Gallions Mount Primary School
Gordonbrock Junior School
Grasmere Primary School
Harrington Hill Primary School
Horn Park Infant School
Meadowgate School
Pilgrims Way Primary School
Riverside Primary School
Shapla Primary School
St James Primary School (Southwark)
Thomas Buxton Infant School
Wix Primary School

We thank the following schools which have given us permission to use photographs of their classrooms.
Bannockburn Primary School
Berger Junior School
Blue Gate Fields Infant School
Columbia Primary School
Dorothy Gardener Nursery School
Michael Faraday Primary School
Grasmere Primary School
Meadowgate School
Shaftesbury Park Primary School
Shapla Primary School
St James Primary School (Southwark)
St Paul's Whitechapel C.E. J.M.I. School
Wix School

Understanding reading: an introduction

Over the past twenty years there has been a rapid growth in our knowledge of the reading process. This information has had implications for teaching and learning; schools are more concerned than they once were about the quality of the books they offer to children in the very early stages of learning to read. There is a move towards providing children with good literary experiences from the outset, and many schools now use children's picture books as a central part of the reading programme provided in the classroom: the so-called 'real books' movement. This move is not a return to earlier teaching approaches such as 'look and say'. It reflects developments in reading theory, developments which make it necessary for teachers to review all aspects of their practice in this area, including the books that will make up children's first reading experiences in school. In this introduction we list some of the influences that have brought about changes in practice. Both here, and in the rest of the book, we discuss some of the issues that those teachers who have found the kinds of structures available in reading schemes inadequate have had to face in constructing an effective alternative framework for their practice.

Reading continues to be a subject of controversy, and to take up space in the media. There is a persistent tendency to polarise questions of reading instruction into diametrically opposed and simplified positions (phonics *or* look-and-say; reading schemes *or* real books). Television and the media trivialise the subject by setting up artificial debates between people who are expected to defend fixed points of view. The solution to this polarisation is often said to lie in 'mixed methods', in which elements from all of these simplified approaches are blended in a reading curriculum.

It seems that people would prefer reading to be simple: a simple and easily definable activity with simple ways of learning how to do it. But reading is not a simple activity; it is one of the mind's most complex accomplishments. Even in 1908, the psychologist E.B. Huey was outlining the size of the task involved in defining reading:

And so to completely analyze what we do when we read would almost be the acme of a psychologist's achievements, for it would be to describe very many of the most intricate workings of the human mind as well as to unravel the tangled story of the most remarkable specific performance that civilization has learned in all its history."

More recently, a cognitive psychologist has described reading as "externally guided thinking" (Neisser 1967), a description which goes some way towards suggesting the complexity of the process, and explaining why simple minimal definitions of it are unhelpful. This description emphasises the active and cognitive elements in reading, and its continuously developing nature, as well as underlining the role of the text in the reading process.

The quest for meaning

Reading is much more than the decoding of black marks upon a page: it is a quest for meaning and one which requires the reader to be an active participant."

English for ages 5-16, Chapter 16.2

We have learned a great deal about reading over the past twenty years, and are in a better position now to appreciate the accomplishment involved in learning to read, and also to see how ready the mind is to take on this new learning. Many researchers, writers, teachers and theorists have enlarged our understanding of the reading process.

Some of the most fundamental insights came from linguists studying language development, from cognitive psychologists, and from psycholinguists. Studies of language acquisition and development showed young children's rapid growth as language users, and the developing rule systems that they use on their way to a control of the full adult grammar. Linguists like Halliday (1975) stressed the interactive nature of language development, and the way in which adults help children to take part in human conversations, and to use language in order to express their own meanings. The links between language development and literacy development began to be made, and psycholinguists like Frank Smith and Kenneth Goodman brought the insights of cognitive psychology to the study of the reading process. Cognitive psychologists saw learning as an active process: the mind in a constant search to make sense of the environment around it. The psycholinguists saw readers similarly engaged in an active meaning-making process, using every available cue to make sense of the text on the page. Goodman's miscue inventory, by analyzing the information provided by reader's guesses and errors, demonstrated how many different sources of information readers draw on in their quest for meaning.

Teachers took several lessons from the psycholinguists. They learned above all to regard errors as information, and to be more analytical in their approach to hearing children read. They understood more about the different kinds of knowledge - linguistic and semantic as well as grapho-phonic - that children were drawing on in their quest for meaning and learned how to help them to use these different cueing systems in their reading. And they became aware that readers operating in this way needed texts which would encourage them to guess and predict, and which would enable them to use the full range of their knowledge.

Culture, society and literacy

At the same time, some linguists with an interest in social issues were beginning to look at the way in which language and communications are affected by social settings, and by social position. Valuable studies by Margaret Clark (1976), in Scotland, and Jane Torrey (1973), in Chicago, considered the development of children who could read before they went to school. These 'young fluent readers' were not by any means all middle class children but they had had ready access to print, or books, and support of various kinds from their parents. In the Scottish research, books (often library books) were around in the home, and reading was a normal activity in the families studied. Girls and boys seemed to have somewhat different interests in learning to read and in the books they turned to. The black working-class child in the Chicago study appeared, according to his family, to have taught himself to read from the television.

Since these studies, Gordon Wells' extended Bristol research project has provided a much fuller picture of the way in which early language experiences lay the foundations for literacy learning, and has found a strong positive link between children's early experiences of story and of being read to, and their later progress in schooled literacy.

Sociolinguistics studied language, not in the abstract, but in real human social situations. Jane Torrey applied Goodman's miscue analysis to the reading of black American children, and found that their miscues were perfectly consistent with the grammar of their speech. Her work, and the work of other sociolinguists, suggests that schools may not always recognise the linguistic accomplishments of children who speak a dialect different from the mainstream dialect, or whose culture is not the mainstream culture.

There has been a growing awareness that all learning takes place in a social context, and that children's attitudes to literacy will reflect their home culture. Shirley Brice Heath's ethnographic study (1983) of two specific communities in Carolina (one working-class white, one rural black) looks at the way in which children's early literacy experiences reflect the different literacy events and patterns of child-rearing in these two communities, and observes what happens when the children go to school in the nearby town. Schieffelin and Cochran Smith (1984) have described how a Sino-Vietnamese boy learnt to read English successfully in an American school although his home appeared to offer little means of extending his reading experience, and he was learning in a second language. They attribute his success to the fact that literacy was an inherent part of his home culture, and that success was both assumed, and valued.

There is still a great deal to learn about the links between literacy, culture and class. One of the problems about research in this area is that it is most frequently carried out by white middle class researchers, and there is a constant problem of bias entering the obser-vations and judgments made. But sociolinguistics has been helpful to teachers in alerting them to the importance of culturally appropriate materials – books which speak directly to children's own cultural and linguistic experience – and also in making them aware of the importance of under-standing more about children's home experiences and making closer links with homes.

Literacy at home and at school

A third crucial influence on thinking about reading, has been a recent spate of studies of children's pre-school literacy learning. Often these have been studies by parents of their own children. Such researchers and writers as Glenda Bissex (1980), Dorothy Butler (1988), Hugh and Maureen Crago (1983), Marcia Bhagban (1984), Shirley Payton (1984) and Carol Fox (1984) have greatly illuminated our picture of children's awareness of literacy in the pre-school years, and have revealed a wealth of experience and knowledge acquired before children begin

school. It is true that these writers are, again, mainly white and middle-class, but the weight of the evidence that they offer for very young children's capacity for intense involvement in story, literary experiences, and reading and writing, is impressive.

This testimony from parent-researchers has supported the work of the psycholinguists and sociolinguists, by showing that the acquisition of literacy is part of children's development as language users in a literate society, by demonstrating how 'literacy events' are continually occuring in any social context, and by analysing how children learn from them. Teachers have gained a great deal from this evidence of the learning that children do before they come to school. It is now quite im-possible to imagine that children know nothing about reading or writing before they enter the reception class, or even the nursery. The need to recognise the learning that has already gone on at home, and to ensure that school learning builds on home learning, rather than ignoring it, is now much more generally accepted in schools, and has obvious implications for practice.

There is a need for closer partnerships with parents, and for home-school links in which teachers learn from parents about their children's literacy experiences, as well as informing them about progress in school. The discussion with parents in the *Primary Language Record* provides an occasion for sharing such information. In the case of bilingual children, such a sharing is particularly crucial, for children may be becoming literate in more than one language, and it will be important to be aware of the literacy experiences in the first language that children will be drawing on in learning to read in English.

Why stories matter

Finally, a growing body of evidence had pointed to the crucial part that texts can play in children's development as readers. Evidence from homes and classrooms, again frequently provided by parents and by teachers themselves, has emphasised the role of the texts themselves in learning to read. Favourite books which children return to again and again are often a major factor in their learning, and all teachers and parents have stories about books which have played this role for particular children. Don Holdaway, in *The Foundations of Literacy* (1979), drew on these kinds of experiences in developing his 'bedtime story model' of a reading curriculum, in which children were given the opportunity to revisit favourite stories and make them part of their developing repertoire as readers. Henrietta Dombey (1984) has looked at how good teachers help children to enjoy the experience of being read to, and to make personal sense of the narratives in books. She finds strong continuities between home and school experience in this area. Margaret Meek (1988) has described certain texts as 'texts that teach', and has looked at the many 'untaught lessons' that children learn from the texts themselves. She points out that much of the knowledge that children need to make sense of narrative is never directly taught, and that the writers and artists who produce books for children are often some of their most important teachers in this respect.

One of the strongest forces that leads children to make sense of reading is the sense of story that we all have. In *The Cool Web* (1977), Barbara Hardy suggests that making up stories is something that we all do continuously - a 'primary act of mind'. We make sense of experience through turning it into story; we remember and dream in story. Small children engage in long whispered dialogues with an imaginary other in bed or under the table, making up fantasies and stories. They develop a knowledge about story from the stories they are read and told and see on television. It is this desire to create stories that children bring to making sense of written text. Frank Smith calls this 'world-making', and it is what the mind is uniquely able to do.

Teachers who appreciate the essential role that satisfying stories can have in children's development as readers want to provide the best possible reading experiences in their classrooms. The move to a literature-based reading curriculum has come about because of the strong belief that children should have access, from the very beginnings of reading in school, to the impressive range of literature for young children now available. Teachers like Jill Bennett (1991) and Liz Waterland (1988) have written about the role that such picture story books can play in children's learning to read, and about the very important place that reading aloud to children has in their learning.

What the reader knows

Reading, then, is a very complex achievement, and when children learn to read they draw on a range of different kinds of knowledge and experience – linguistic, semantic, social, cultural, narrative, literate and literary. Of course, some of the knowledge that they draw on is grapho-phonic knowledge, a knowledge of the written code, or of how we 'draw speech' in Vygotsky's phrase. Children will need to know how sounds are represented in writing, and about the alphabetic system. This knowledge of grapho-phonic relationships is, however, in itself insufficient to enable children to learn to read (though it may enable them to decode print to sound, sometimes rather slowly and painfully).

Children have a considerable appetite for knowledge of the grapho-phonic system and are often quick to recognise letters from their name and to see patterns of letters. Anne Washtell's study of her reception infant class (1989) shows them constantly engaged in this kind of activity. Teachers can feed this kind of curiosity and stimulate children's interest in the writing system in all kinds of ways – through shared reading and writing sessions, through compiling displays and word banks, through word games, through alphabet books and books involving word play. Careful record-keeping will reveal whether children are drawing on their grapho-phonic knowledge or not, and whether they need encouraging to do so.

Grapho-phonic knowledge alone will not enable a child to learn to read, and nor will just reading them stories necessarily enable them to take on the reading process for themselves. The beginning reader has to learn to bring together different kinds of knowledge and to draw on the different kinds of cues available to them in texts. Some psychologists and psycholinguists have considered this process and suggested how these different kinds of knowledge are combined in the act of reading. David Rumelhart (1976) produced a 'parallel processing' model of reading to explain how readers are able to draw on all the different kinds of information that enable them to make sense of texts. In a critique of 'bottom-up' psychological models of reading, which assume that reading is a question of combining low-level information, letter by letter, or word by word, he presented an *interactive* model which imagines readers drawing on a range of knowledge sources at a number of levels, from high level semantic and syntactic levels, to lower levels of information such as knowledge about word and letter features. He describes the act of reading as a continual oscillation between these higher and lower levels, with hypotheses set up at one level being confirmed or rejected at another.

High level information – the big shapes

We now know a great deal more about what Rumelhart terms the 'high-level information units' and what we might call the 'big shapes' in texts. These larger overarching textual structures – such as different kinds of narrative structures, and the structures that relate to different genres – and the way these are reflected in the rhythms and tunes of written language, are a most important source of knowledge, which readers have to draw on, in addition to their sense of the unfolding meaning of a text, to support their reading. Young readers who are already developing, from being read to, a sensitive ear for the rhythms, tunes and textual structures of texts, learn to be aware of such structures in written language. A feeling for such 'big shapes', as well as a memory of what the text says, serves as a helpful framework for their reading of the words on the page. The 'tune on the page' plays an important part in supporting children's reading.

Traditional reading instruction, and 'phonics' teaching, put all the emphasis on 'low-level' information and did not recognise the importance of larger textual structures in the learning to read process. But studies of young readers 'reenactments' of familiar texts (Holdaway 1979) suggest that some readers develop an awareness of such structures at a very early age indeed. At some point, however, all readers have to begin to draw on information from all of these different sources, and match their growing knowledge of the print with their sense of the whole, and their understanding of the meaning.

The orchestration of knowledge

A recent and important American study by a group of researchers from the Educational Testing Service has provided a most helpful description of reading, which respects the different kinds of knowledge that are involved in the reading process. In *Inquiry into Meaning (1985)* reading is defined as:

'the act of orchestrating diverse knowledge in order to construct meaning from text while maintaining reasonable fluency and reasonable accountability to the information contained in the writing. . . the act begins when the knowledge is orchestrated.'

These different kinds of knowledge range from 'a knowledge of literary styles and rhythms' to knowledge of 'phonetic information and letter-sound correspondence'.

The researchers in *Inquiry into Meaning* studied forty inner-city children, of whom two thirds were black, in their extended classroom-based project. The case studies in the book are fascinating in their descriptions of the children's individual styles of learning, and the different paths they take to reading, and we draw on them later in this book. However, the project workers did draw some general conclusions from their data. Among these conclusions was a broad distinction that the researchers felt they could draw between those young readers in their study who obviously flavoured *fluency* in their reading, and who preferred to maintain the flow of reading and attend to the overall meaning of the text, and others who favoured *accuracy*, focused their attention rather narrowly, and read in a step-by-step way, sometimes being unwilling to proceed if they could not identify a word. About half of the children studied seemed to fall into one of these two categories.

The researchers did not find that a preference for either fluency or accuracy was related in any systematic way to the children's reading progress; they came to see these differences as style differences in children's approach to their learning in this area. In time most of the children came to achieve greater balance in their reading. Those who read fluently but sometimes inaccurately slowed down and

came to pay more attention to the local details of text; those who read haltingly and accurately came to read more fluently, and to make errors which showed they were attending to cues in the text other than the print cues.

A significant parallel can be drawn between these findings and the interactive model of the reading process described earlier. It seems likely that the young readers characterised as favouring fluency were responding more directly to the larger shapes – or 'higher information units' – in texts, while those favouring accuracy were inclined to focus on smaller 'low-level' units. If this connection seems valid, then we can begin to formulate an interesting and complex theory about learning to read, one which respects both the range of information contained within a text, and the differences between individual learners.

'Either/or' theories of learning to read have not got us very far in thinking about reading. They have tended to polarise debate, and also to polarise practice. They also fail to reflect the complexity of the learning to read process – the different kinds of knowledge that are basic to the process, the need to achieve a balance and integration between them, and the need for teachers to help children to use their different stylistic strengths. The ability to read is not located in any one individual aspect of reading, such as a sense of book language, or a knowledge of print, but in the whole activity, when these different aspects are orchestrated. And, as in any skilled process, practice is essential to the achievement of this balance and orchestration.

Supportive texts

A further major finding in *Inquiry into Meaning* was that certain kinds of texts appeared to be supporting children's early reading more effectively than others. The researchers were particularly impressed by the way in which children showed a sensitivity to literary styles and rhythms, and noticed that their reading seemed to be supported by texts that rhymed (such as many of the Dr. Seuss books) and by writing which has a musical patterning, or a rhythmic flow. Several children seemed to read texts with these literary qualities more expressively and easily than was typical of their early reading. This is important evidence, and suggests that there is a great deal more to be discovered about the kinds of books that are likely to be significant for children learning to read – a subject that is of fundamental interest to teachers developing a reading curriculum. The question of the role of the text in learning to read and reading is the subject of a later chapter in this book.

The book is divided into two main parts. In Part One we focus on four major partners in the learning to read process: the children themselves, their parents, their teachers, and the books that form part of their early reading experiences. Any approach to teaching reading now would have to take into account the different roles that these partners play in helping children learn. In this part of the book we look at what each partner brings to the learning process, and draw on recent research and first hand accounts to describe and analyse their contributions more fully.

In Part Two we look more closely at practical approaches to the teaching of reading and review the different elements that need to be included in a comprehensive reading policy. We look at ways of implementing what we now know about reading, and at the kind of teaching approaches that will be most effective in supporting children's learning. We consider how reading policies can reflect equal opportunities policies; how children from all social and linguistic backgrounds can gain more equal access to reading and books. We discuss ways of supporting children with reading difficulties, and of keeping track of children's progress and development in reading. Throughout this part of the book we have drawn on the help of teachers who have shared their knowledge and expertise with us, and their classrooms are featured in the many photographs that illustrate the approaches we describe.

In Part One of The Reading Book we focus on the partners in the reading process – the children, their parents, their teachers, and the texts they meet – and consider the part they play in learning to read. Between the chapters, we observe 'A Day in the Life' of three young readers.

Children learning to read

'From the earliest stages children derive great pleasure from sharing books and listening to stories. Primary schools must have a clear policy and whole school approach to the teaching of reading which builds success for all children so that they clearly identify themselves as young readers who find pleasure in books'.

English for ages 5-16

Children learning to read

To understand more about how children learn to read and what is the key to their learning, we need to reflect on what that learning looks like, in action. We can make a start by looking at teachers' descriptions of children as readers and at accounts of how children see themselves as readers. In recent years more descriptions of this rich and detailed kind have become available because teachers' records are becoming more narrative in character. Records like this are based both on regular and careful observation and on conversations with children. They can therefore take account of children's language and literacy experiences at home and in the community as well as at school.

When we study such records and descriptions, the conclusions we can draw are generally of two main kinds. What we learn contributes to either:

a picture of a common set of key experiences which seem to be influential in the development of most readers

or:

knowledge of the patterns of learning that are particular to individual children, and of the experiences and routines that have supported their learning

In the sections that follow we look at five children learning to read. The descriptions of their learning come from different sources – two are from classroom-based research, while three are taken from teachers' records. These accounts highlight the fact that there is a common pattern to children's learning, and also reflect the children's individual styles as learners.

One of the most detailed observation-based studies of reading to date is reported in *Inquiry into Meaning: An Investigation of Learning to Read* (1985). This book was the result of a six-year American research project, which focused on young children's differences as learners rather than on ways of teaching reading. The aim was to discover more about children learning to read in the context of their classrooms, to explore their developing understandings of the reading process and, through case studies, to identify their preferred styles of learning.

In this chapter we look briefly at the early reading history of Carrie - the focus of one of the detailed case studies. In the extract below, which is part of the summary of Carrie's development, a number of formative statements are made, statements that describe significant aspects of her reading behaviour. The phrases in italics relate to the analysis that follows this extract.

Carrie *from* Inquiry into Meaning

'Midway in the kindergarten year, Carrie initiates her first attempts to read. As with most undertakings, *she approaches reading with confidence* and resourcefulness and apparently sees the task to be not so much a question of 'learning to read' ads of 'starting to read'. *She plunges directly into the matter, insisting that her teacher, parents, others, read to and with her.* In her first 'readings' to the teacher, *she relies principally upon memory for the story,* aided by picture clues and a willingness to ad-lib. Although she soon begins to draw reliably on information encoded in print, acquiring word analysis skills along the way, *her confidence in reading and her allegiance to the story line remain firm throughout the record. She never goes through a phase of word calling or of attending excessively to letter sounds.* Her progress is steady, with no evidence that learning leaps forward or is suddenly transformed. By the conclusion of first grade, she is a competent young reader firmly in control of the reading process and able to branch out into a variety of books'

The researchers noted that there were certain patterns or themes which could be identified in seven-year-old Carrie's reading record and analysed them under four major headings:

Confidence and persistence in beginning reading
"If she doesn't know the words she will make them up. Nothing gets in the way."

Familiarisation and rereading
"He (Carrie's dad) told me that she is after him all the time to read . . . and she says to read it again . . . the next day, she'll want him to read the same book yet again."

Memory and anticipation of narrative
"If you read her a story she will 'read' (tell) the story back to you . . . she can retell a story from only hearing it once."

Capitalising upon contexts for reading: people and settings
"She takes the role of sort of a leader. For example, one of her friends will ask me, "Can Carrie read this book to me?""

It is of great interest to note how Carrie adapts her patterns of behaviour as her independence as a reader increases. The teacher comments on the fact that throughout her first year and a half of schooling, Carrie would go out of her way to create opportunities for being read to and reading with others. Over twenty four people (adults and children) are recorded as having read with Carrie in her first year at school. However, toward the end of her second year there was a notable shift in this pattern, when she began to read alone.

"She does not grab visitors to read to, the way she did."

The need for Carrie to have an audience had diminished. She no longer found it so necessary to practise aloud as she grew in independence as a reader. Moreover, she could now branch out and read a wider range of texts.

Observations of this kind serve more than one purpose:

- they represent individual children's patterns of learning
- they highlight the range and variety of experiences that contribute to children's development
- they enable us to document children's progress and development over time.

The research reported in *Inquiry into Meaning* was an ambitious longitudinal study, and produced powerful evidence. Though there has been no comparable research in the U.K., there have been, nevertheless, some interesting projects concerned with children's learning to read, where the focus has been on the affective nature of learning as well as the cognitive, and where texts have been considered as central to the process.

David *from* Reading for Real

In 1987 a group of teachers in Croydon contributed to an occasional paper entitled *Communications Developmental Learning Reading in the Early Years*. The paper was compiled by Lynda Yard, the Advisory teacher for Language Development, and it provides a framework for observing children's developing reading. It includes a record sheet in two parts. One part refers to 'Attitude to Reading', the other considers 'Developing strategies, knowledge and understanding'.

An important prefatory statement at the head of the record reads:

This record sheet is intended to be used simply as a guide. We emphasise that we believe emergent reading follows no linear progression and that the sequence of development is unique for each child

This emphasis on the uniqueness of individual learning patterns helps teachers as they plan for children's further development. The record directs observation to a wide range of early reading behaviours, from a sense of story to attention to print, and this enables teachers to look back and see what factors in a child's experience seem to be making a difference to their learning to read.

Date	Book	Child's strengths	Teacher strategies
17 Sept	Smarty Pants	He read it well, pointing as he read. He was proud of himself. Read with care.	I asked him to point.
25 Sept	Smarty Pants	He obviously enjoys this book. Read with care. He managed the rhymes, which meant reading ahead.	I looked at rhyming words with him.
19 Oct	Smarty Pants	Read really well; pointing with care. Remembered to include reading ahead to make words rhyme. Could point to 'Smarty Pants' and 'see me'	Asked him to show me 'Smarty Pants' and the 'see me' all throughout the book

The extract *(left)* from a chapter by Lynda Yard in *Reading for Real* quotes from a Croydon teacher's diary for a Year 1 child, David. These diary entries enable us to observe which books he chose to share with the teacher, the range of strategies he used when reading aloud, and the kind of help the teacher offered on each occasion. The entries are highly specific but together they pinpoint some important factors in David's growth as a reader.

Between 17th September and 19th October of the year covered by the record, David chose to read *Smarty Pants* on three separate occasions with his teacher. Lynda Yard comments:

At the beginning of the year the books David chose to share were ones he knew well with lots of rhyme and repetition; he chose one three times as he gradually gained in confidence.

A month later *The Monster's Party* became a frequent favourite and the teacher's notes show clearly the interplay between the text, the child and the teacher.

His teacher commented on the way to read the book on each occasion:

Very confident.

Super, fluent confident reading.

Read with assurance.

and on the strategies he had used and his growing ability to identify individual words:

managed to pick out 'monster' 'fly' and 'can' with no help. Self-correcting now.

pointing as he read. Could tell me he knew the word 'dance' because it began with a 'd'.

We gain insight into the teacher's role, both from the way she comments on his strengths and from the way she intervenes. Since the beginning of the term she had encouraged David to point to the words on the page as he reenacted the story from memory, and built on his interest in texts with a rhythmic quality. She had also encouraged him in building a sight vocabulary.

Three months later we learn that David is increasing the repertoire of familiar books that he shares with the teacher. The majority come from the *Story Chest* series and are ones that he would have known well from group reading sessions. Another dimension to David's learning becomes apparent as his confidence grows in the summer months. He chooses to read to a greater number of children and adults in school – he senses the pleasure of sharing story and gives himself many opportunities for practice.

If we look at the four major themes that were identified in Carrie's early development, we can see meaningful comparisons that can be made between the two children's learning patterns. As with Carrie, *confidence and persistence* go hand in hand for David; one attribute supports the other as his competence increases. A growing *familiarity with a group of favourite stories,* which he frequently chooses to read and reread to the teacher, is the basis for his learning; in David's case the texts chosen are often ones marked by lots of rhyme and repetition. *The memorisation of these favourite narratives* supports his reading and his developing knowledge of how print works; in the context of this kind of reading he begins to be able to identify individual words and letter sounds.

Date	Book	Child's strengths	Teacher strategies
16 Nov	The Monster's Party	Very confident, managed to pick out 'monster' 'fly' and 'can' with no help. Self-correcting now.	Asked him for some words.
30 Nov	The Monster's Party	Super, fluent confident reading. Read with assurance. Likes story because of the monster and also because he had his birthday party on Saturday.	Asked him why he likes this book. I enjoyed it.
11 Dec	The Monster's Party	Read well, pointing as he read. Could tell me he knew the word 'dance' because it began with a 'd'	Asked him to point. Asked him to show me 'monster'

In one respect David and Carrie differ somewhat in their reading behaviour. For both of them, *reading to and with other people* is a key activity. But whereas Carrie will involve anybody and everybody in her learning to read from the outset, seizing every opportunity to practice with adults and children at first, and only gradually ceasing to need this kind of interactive support for her learning, David's development is different. His growing independence is marked by his increased confidence in reading with others, so that while the number of Carrie's partners in the reading process declines in the period covered by her record, the number of people mentioned in David's record increases.

The Primary Language Record

Most of what we have come to know about children learning to read in recent years, is a direct result of what Yetta Goodman has termed 'kid-watching': record-keeping based on observation. The development of the *Primary Language Record* has enabled the collection of a mass of evidence about children as readers. This evidence includes teachers' observations and records of their discussions with parents and children.

Children's learning to read has to be seen in the context of their total language and learning development in and outside school, and it is useful to be able to look at

- the preferred contexts for reading
- the people who have supported development
- the texts that have made a difference
- the range of opportunities and experiences that have influenced progress.

It is the combination of these kinds of information that helps us to describe the complex process of individual's learning to read, and to understand what constitutes evidence of progress and development.

The *Primary Language Record* offers teachers ways of looking and analysing their observations, initially through the diary of observations and the reading samples, and subsequently provides a framework for recording aspects of development.

Alison: the reading diary

The reading diary enables teachers to note observations about a child's reading which seem significant. Often, however, the full significance of these notes is not realised until a number of entries have been made, when a pattern often emerges.

In the following example from the record of Alison, a Year 1 girl, it is possible to see definite patterns in her behaviour as a reader, to make generalisations about what she knows and how she uses this knowledge, and about the social nature of her reading.

This information could be described in more detail under three headings:

How she feels about herself as a reader

Alison is confident in talking about the texts that she likes and knows and is gaining in independence as a reader as her experience of reading in a range of contexts increases.

What she knows and can do

She knows a number of rhymes and jingles, many of which she has learned at school. She is building up a repertoire of known texts and choosing to read this collection frequently. She has clear ideas about how she prefers to organise this rereading e.g. 'Often chooses a book where there is more than one copy of

---

2 Reading and Writing: diary of observations
(reading and writing in English and/or other community languages)

Dates	Reading
	Record actual examples of the child's reading (including wider experiences of story) across a range of contexts.
13 1 87	Knows many rhymes & jingles from 'To Market' and 'Bibbili bonty' Storychest rhyme books. 'If I Had a Donkey' 'Mary lost her foal' plus a number of playground rhymes. Often will choose 'big books' picture books as well as Storychest to read with 2 or 3 friends. Will often repeat catchphrases out of context, applying them to life experiences. When asked to leave an activity for a moment to do something else, she said, 'If I look round I'll forget' – a refrain from a favourite book.
27 1 87	First thing in the morning, before the register is taken, A. sorts out the book she is going to read with a friend. Often chooses a book where there is more than one copy of the same.
4 2 87	A read a shared-writing book 'The Paper-bag Princess' to a group of friends first thing this morning.

the same'. There are signs that she is beginning to relate what she reads to her everyday experiences - the early stages of reflectiveness.

Her preferred contexts for reading

Alison's reading is a highly social activity and the record shows her regularly choosing to read with friends, and setting up these shared reading sessions.

The reading sample in the next example shows another way of looking. Here a Sylheti and English speaking child (also in Year 1) is reading aloud a familiar text – *What's the time Mr.Wolf?* by Colin Hawkins (Picture Lions). The teacher used this situation to take a running record, details of which are printed below.

The running record has helped the teacher to look more closely at how a young child like Khaleda approaches the reading of a text she knows reasonably well. In addition to gauging how the child reads aloud, and how she responds to a chosen text, this kind of assessment makes it possible to ascertain in detail how she tackles print. It provides an opportunity to take stock of Khaleda's strengths and analyse her miscues.

The sample enables the teacher to reflect on what she has learned from the running record. She notes that Khaleda is an independent-minded reader who persists with the text and only needs actual help on one occasion. The teacher

The reading sample

3 **Reading Samples** (reading in English and/or oth	
to include reading aloud and reading silently	
Dates	
Title or book/text (fiction or information)	What's the time Mr Wolf?
Known/unknown text	Known
Sampling procedure used: informal assessment/running record/miscue analysis	Running Record
Overall impression of the child's reading: • confidence and degree of independence • involvement in the book/text • the way in which the child read the text aloud	Very confident and independent. Only needed support on one occasion. Determined to make the text make sense. Pays attention to detail.
Strategies the child used when reading aloud: • drawing on previous experience to make sense of the book/text • playing at reading • using book language • reading the pictures • focusing on print (directionality, 1:1 correspondence, recognition of certain words) • using semantic/syntactic/grapho-phonic cues • predicting • self-correcting • using several strategies or over-dependent on one	Drew on her knowledge of reading another well-known text - Hairy Bear. This was a fine example of K. using a range of strategies in order to read accurately and fluently. Using a running record has highlighted her ability to use all she knows about two languages in order to read in English. She self-corrected on many occasions.
Child's response to the book/text: • personal response • critical response (understanding, evaluating, appreciating wider meanings)	It is a favourite book and she likes to read it on her own and with friends.
What this sample shows about the child's development as a reader. **Experiences/support needed to further development.**	The text supports her development. There is much evidence to show how she is using so many strategies not least of which is her knowledge of two languages.
• *Early indicators that the child is moving into reading*	

thinks that Khaleda may be drawing on her knowledge of patterns of language in both her languages to read the text: she tries out some structures that do not quite work, but has a good developing sense of how the English text should sound, and soon self-corrects. Khaleda corrects her reading on a number of occasions, sometimes more than once on one piece of the text. On these occasions she tries out a variety of strategies, from reading mainly for meaning to focusing on initial sounds.

The sample form has structured the teacher's way of thinking about Khaleda's reading, and has also given her important information to use about what is involved in learning to read. Together with the insights provided by the running record, it has given her a detailed snapshot of a child's reading on a particular day with a specific text. Sampling like this contributes valuably to our understanding of how children become increasingly competent as readers. It is also important to see this example in the context of previous samples, and of classroom observations of the same child's reading. Only in this way can a complete picture be gained.

B2 Reading *(Handbook pages 23-28)*

Please comment on the child's progress and development as a reader in English and/or other community languages: the stage at which the child is operating (refer to the reading scales on pages 26-27); the range, quantity and variety of reading in all areas of the curriculum; the child's pleasure and involvement in story and reading, alone or with others; the range of strategies used when reading and the child's ability to reflect critically on what is read.

At beginning of Spring term B. showed little interest in books and was very reluctant to read with an adult often, saying that, he didn't want to. He sat attentively during group reading of 'Big Books' but rarely joined in. By the end of Jan. however he had learnt Mrs. Wishy Washy off by heart and he gradually grew in confidence and started to take risks with other books both on his own and with an adult, often readily choosing to read in the book area. He regularly takes books home. He has now built up a collection

B2 (continued) of books that he knows well— Hairy Bear, Not IV ow Bernard, If you meet a Dragon, Jigaree etc. They are mainly story chest & this is of his own choosing. He likes making his own books and he often chooses to read these — the message stays constant. By the end of the term he was pointing from left to right as he read. He was just beginning to focus in more closely on the text of these well known books & showing one to one correspondence + also attempting to sound out the initial sounds of words he was unsure of e.g. crim cram cross em bim bam beadem Tom Hairy Bear.

What experiences and teaching have helped/would help development in this area? Record outcomes of any discussion with head teacher, other staff, or parent(s).

In March he started to take home information books about our class topic on Bears and seemed very interested in them. He knows his letters and sounds and needs to be encouraged to use this knowledge as another means of helping him with the text when he got stuck.

(His is non-fluent reader (2) on Reading scale.

Barry: the main record

Evidence of children's degree of involvement and experience in reading, gathered in the ways described above, can then be recorded in a summative way on to the *Part B2 section of the main record*. The record shown for Barry, who is five years old, is taken from this section. Barry's language is English and he is in the Reception year at the time of this account. It is only his first term at school, and yet there is already a significant range of information about his reading development. If we analyse the teacher's comments, we can identify different kinds of information in the record, all of which can inform our understanding of the processes involved in learning to read.

Opportunities and experiences that have been important to him

• Listening to stories, poems etc. being read aloud – often the same ones, over and over again.

• Shared reading from 'big books', joining in where text is known.

• Opportunity to grow in confidence and experience before being expected to perform as an individual reader.

• Having time to browse among the books, to choose freely and to take favourite books home.

• Reading with a number of adults as he became more willing to take risks.

• Making connections between reading and writing through composing own stories/texts and making own books.

Specific strategies for making sense of print (known text)

• Pointing from left to right as he reads.

• Beginning to show one-to-one correspondence with some known pieces of text.

• Attempting to sound out initial sounds of some unfamiliar words. Awareness of repeated initial sounds.

Resources that have played a part in B's learning to read;

- *Mrs. Wishy Washy; Harry Bear; Not Now Bernard; If you Meet a Dragon; Jigaree* and many others from *Story Chest*. Books he has made in the class-room and information books on bears – directly linked to a class project.

- The classroom teacher, other adults and children in school, and his parents have all played a part in his learning.

The teacher's initial comment about Barry's attitude to books and reading in his first few weeks at school deserves particular attention: 'At beginning of Spring term Barry showed little interest in books and was very reluctant to read with an adult . . .' This comment or comments like it are familiar. In a variety of ways they appear on the records of a number of children. Often these children are boys.

Boys do not do as well overall as girls in reading (or writing) in primary schools. There may be a number of reasons for this, many of them firmly embedded in the hidden curriculum. They could include the attitudes of teachers, parents, society and the children themselves. Book provision in schools and classrooms may also play its part in influencing attitudes to reading. Who chooses the books, what books are provided, and do they reflect the interests of boys as well as girls? Is there a balance between fiction and information books? Such issues need to be addressed where observation reveals clear differences between girls' and boys' progress as readers.

B3 Writing *(Handbook pages 29-31)*

Please comment on the child's progress and development as a writer in English and/or other community languages: the degree of confidence and independence as a writer; the range, quantity and variety of writing in all areas of the curriculum; the child's pleasure and involvement in writing both narrative and non-narrative, alone and in collaboration with others; the influence of reading on the child's writing; growing understanding of written language, its conventions and spelling.

At beginning of term B could confidently write his name – christian + surname using capital letters. He began to attempt lower case after seeing his namecard. By the end of January he was writing a string of letters to represent long the message. He used a variety of letters outside of his name. Gradually he began to use initial sounds + also showed signs of hearing the end sound too when given help. He became very keen to use the writing area and spontaneously produced his own little storybooks mainly about a man with big ears which he found highly amusing – so did the other children when he read them to them! The books were well sequenced both in text + illustration. He always took them home.

What experiences and teaching have helped/would help development in this area? Record outcomes of any discussion with lead teacher, other staff, or parent(s).

He is gradually building up a basic sight vocab. of words he knows & he is just beginning to use these in his writing.✓
It is very important that B is able to continue to produce his spontaneous storybooks by being able to readily use the writing area where he can take risks.

To understand fully children's progress as readers it seems essential to chart development within a broad framework such as that offered by the multi-dimensional record-keeping of the *Primary Language Record*, where talking and listening, reading, and writing are given equal importance in a child's language development. In the case of Barry, the B3 (Writing) section of his main record enables us to look at the teacher's assessment of him as a writer and to note the interfunctional nature of literacy learning – the way in which his learning to read supports his learning to write and vice versa.

Encouraging Barry to compose his own texts has supported his emerging understanding of how readers and writers behave, and of how the English writing system operates. It is through writing that he seems to gain initial confidence about himself as a learner, and the pleasure that he derives from his success is soon generalised to his learning to read.

The evidence collected in this way serves to future teaching and inform the assessment of children's growth as readers; it is the basis of true formative assessment.

In this chapter we have considered five young readers in order to learn more about learning to read. The details of their experiences and achievements given here reveal common factors in their learning, but also some differences between them as learners. Before we conclude this chapter by considering the key common factors that seem to run through their reading experiences, we will look briefly at their individual learning styles.

One difference that has already been mentioned concerns children's readiness to read to and with other people. Some children, like Carrie, are social readers from the start, they take every chance they get to share books with others, and, like Alison, they will initiate these occasions for shared reading. Others, like David and Barry, are less confident initially and may need more time sharing books one-to-

Differences in learning styles

one with the teacher, or taking part in the group reading of Big Books, before they are prepared to risk reading with others.

Another marked difference relates to a readiness to take risks. Carrie is ready to read texts she has heard only once, supported by her astonishing memory for narrative. Other children, like Barry, need to get to know a text well before they are prepared to risk reading it independently. For these children shared reading will be a particularly important and supportive activity. Barry also tends to limit his reading to a particular group of texts, he feels he knows how to read *Story Chest* books and mainly practises with these. David establishes a group of texts, ones marked by rhyme and repetition, which are for him key experiences.

Some of the children correspond closely to the two broad categories of reader described in *Inquiry into Meaning,* which were referred to in the Introduction. Carrie and Alison both seem to focus on the story, and on keeping the story moving. Carrie in particular exhibits a marked preference for fluency in reading; she seems to be drawing all the time on the high-level information units, or 'big shapes', of story structure, narrative style, and the tune of written language. Barry pays close attention to the texts of the books he knows, pointing to the print, showing one-to-one correspondence, and towards the end of his first term in school attempting to sound out initial sounds. Khaleda pays very particular attention to matching what she reads aloud with what she knows about English and about the English grapho-phonic system; her determination to be accountable to the print is evidenced by her careful self-correction.

In order to become competent readers and effective learners, children need to combine both fluency and accuracy in their reading. Their success in doing this will be affected by the support they receive for their attempts to make sense of the reading process. Teachers will need to be sensitive to children's individual styles of learning and support what they are trying to do, as well as gradually moving them on towards the use of a wider set of strategies and cueing systems.

Key experience and common factors

Finally we need to summarise the key experiences and common factors that seem to contribute to all children's growth as readers. All of the following are important, but individual children will obviously pay more attention to some of the experiences than to others.

Being read to from a growing range of books must surely be the single most important support for children's emergent literacy. When teachers and other adults read aloud to children, they give them insights into the pleasures, interests and purposes of reading, demonstrate what is available to read, and help them to become familiar with the shapes and tunes of written language – the big shapes – that will support their early independent reading, and their subsequent focusing on the small shapes of print.

The texts chosen for reading aloud will be of central importance. Texts need to be meaningful and supportive. In the descriptions of these young readers *certain kinds of texts have recurred regularly:* texts with a strong narrative line, texts featuring repetition, texts which are rhythmical or which rhyme, and so on. The role of the text in learning to read will be the subject of a later chapter in this book. For bilingual children, it will be important to be able to find in the classroom *texts written in their community languages*, and to hear these texts read aloud either on tape or by an adult who shares a language with them. The provision of books in all the languages represented in the classroom will demonstrate the value placed on children's cultural and linguistic backgrounds, and will also support their biliteracy.

In *shared reading experiences* involving a group or the whole class, and featuring big books, commercially produced or home-made, there will be an opportunity for young children to play a more participatory role in the reading of a text. Shared reading can also happen when a group of children read with multiple copies of the same text. These texts are likely to be firm favourites, often part of a *core collection* of books that children meet frequently and have every opportunity to get to know really well. In the context of these supported readings of familiar texts children begin to take on more of the reading process for themselves.

Above all children need *to practise reading*, initially with known and familiar texts, and later with a widening range of more challenging books. They may require different kinds of *support for their practice*. Some will be happier reading with and to the teacher or a known adult, others will be prepared to share with other children and adults from an early stage. Taped versions of favourite books, and of the core collection, can also provide support. *Home/school reading schemes* are an important way in which parents and teachers can pool their knowledge of the child's growth as a reader, and ensure a continuity of support between reading at home and reading at school.

Having the time and space both to *browse in the book corner or library*, previewing books, and reading to oneself, is an important experience for all children to have, and so is *talking about books* with teachers and with other children. This kind of discussion is the beginning of critical literacy; children need opportunities to reflect on their reading, to respond personally to what they have read, and to begin to evaluate the books they meet.

Development in reading will be greatly supported by children's *learning to write*. As children realise the interdependent and interfunctional nature of reading and writing, through activities like shared reading and shared writing, *book-making*, and writing their own versions of familiar texts, the knowledge of written language and of the writing system which is basic to learning to write will also support their growing understanding of reading.

Throughout all these experiences, young readers must be encouraged to use a *wide range of strategies* in their reading (predicting, sampling, confirming, self-monitoring and self-correcting), and a *full range of cueing systems*, semantic, syntactic, grapho-phonic. All of these strategies and cueing systems can be *demonstrated* in shared reading sessions, where children can watch the teacher read aloud. Children who tend to draw on only a narrow range of strategies, and use only certain kinds of knowledge (e.g. knowledge of sound-symbol relationships) can be helped to draw on the other knowledge that they have about books and reading, which they may not be making full use of.

Reading is fundamentally a social phenomenon. Early shared experiences are internalised and become the basis of what children can do independently and what they understand reading to be. Everything we know about learning to read suggests that children's attitudes to reading and their feelings about themselves as learners are crucial to this process. Sensitive teachers will observe what aspects of the reading process children are beginning to focus on, and what experiences give them confidence, and will support their attempts. The provision that teachers make for children, the experiences they provide, the resources they make available in the classroom, and the observational records that they keep, will all affect children's learning.

A day in the life of a reader

POLLY

(age 2 years 8 months; languages: English)

Alison Kelly made written observations of her niece in order to discover the range and variety of experiences that she had with books and texts of all kinds in just one day, from early morning until bedtime. It is interesting to note how Polly initiates much of her own learning, and how adults use these opportunities to support her early reading development. Story, books, print and play are all an integral part of her everyday life.

7.00

Brings *I Want my Potty* (Tony Ross) to me to read to her in bed.

7.45

Looks for cereal packet in cupboard, finds Cocoa Pops, notices P for Polly.

10.30

Plays at putting her baby brother to bed on floor. Covers him with a nappy, re-enacts her own bedtime ritual, reads him a story *Mr. Gumpy's Outing* (John Burningham)

Polly:
Mr. Gumpy's riding (looking at cover), Mr, Gumpy's riding now, Mr.Gumpy... "Can I come?" said the chickens, "If you don't squabble". The *children* squabble!

Alison:
Yes.

Polly:
And what do cock...cocks do...cocks? What do cocks do?

Alison:
Let's see.

Polly:
What do cocks do?

Alison:
The, the cow?

Polly:
No, cocks.

Alison:
Where's the cocks. Oh there, there's the chickens. (reads) "Don't flap" said Mr.Gumpy.

Polly:
Don't flap.

Alison:
And there's the cow.

Polly:
What's it do?

Alison:
(reads) ... if you don't trample about.

Polly:
...if you don't trample about. Can I come? If you don't kick. The cow trampled, and the cock, cock, no the hen flapped, the dog teased the cat and the boat tipped, boat tipped and they all go home for tea.

12.00

Makes shopping list in new 'Spot' notebook.

Shouts out "What do we need?" "What sort?" and "Two pounds or three?" (about a lettuce). For each item adds more up and down marks at bottom of a page.

3.00

On way to park we pass a large long-haired dog.

"Look at that big woolly wolf" she says. (Has only met wolves in stories.)

5.00

Plays long game by herself by fireplace with teddy, boots, large cardboard box and colander. Dad comes in and says

"Whatever next Polly?"

Recognises scenario from *Whatever Next?* (Jill Murphy)

6.30

Bedtime story *The Very Hungry Caterpillar* (Eric Carle)

Reading with frequent interruptions as she tries to sort out what salami is e.g. What's that? Is they open yet? Why? (several times) Is it not for children? Have we got some at home?

Then tries to sort out inconsistency in pictures re caterpillar's feet:

Polly:
Did, did the caterpillar eat not with his, his little feet, holding his little feet? Did he not? (the little feet are evident as the caterpillar eats through the holes on the previous pages but doesn't go through the holes on this page)

Alison:
Yes, I expect he held on to the food. Do you think he held on to the food with his little feet?

Polly:
No, he didn't.

Alison:
How did he manage to eat his food?

Polly:
Put in your mouth.

Parents in partnership

> *"Teachers should take account of the important link between home and school, actively encouraging parents to participate and share in their child's reading".*
>
> *English for ages 5-16*

Parents in partnership

It is only in the last ten years or so that schools have developed policies encouraging parents to play a participatory role in their children's literacy development – and in particular their reading. One mother remembers that when her three children were young, it was a very different story:

When my three children were at infant school in the late sixties and early seventies, I remember two indications of the school attitude towards parents. The first was the prominent yellow line which crossed the whole length of the playground leaving a yard or two of space where parents and toddlers could wait for the school day to end. Just in case there was any doubt as to the purpose of this, it was accompanied by a written commandment: NO PARENT BEYOND THIS LINE. The second memory is of deeper significance. The school actually told new parents that they were not to help their children to learn to read; this was to be left 'to the professionals.

Attitudes have gradually been changing as research findings from many sources have shown that children learn first and foremost from the home, and more specifically that children start school already knowing a great deal about literacy (Clark 1976, Wells 1982, Ferreiro and Teberosky 1983, Goelman, Oberg and Smith 1984, Harste, Woodward and Burke 1984). Such research also makes clear that pre-school children do not need to be economically privileged in order to learn about reading and writing, nor do they need to have experienced direct teaching. Rather, their interest in, and enjoyment of, written language needs to have been supported in particular ways.

Studies made by parents of their pre-school children (Bissex 1980; Payton 1984) have provided detailed pictures of their children's growing awareness of literacy and its importance in their lives. Both parents (one American, the other English) were also teachers and therefore brought to their longitudinal studies a background of knowledge about language and literacy learning. These studies were fundamentally important to our understanding of early literacy development and of the multi-faceted nature of such learning.

Of equal significance was the investigation carried out by the American psychologist Jane Torrey (1973), to explore the case of a young black boy who came to school already a competent reader and writer. Torrey writes: "John had entered kindergarten . . . in a large southern city at the age of four years ten months. His teacher discovered that he could both read and write and that he was not interested in doing much else." His mother reported that he had been able to read almost from the time he could talk and yet no one had read to him or taught him to read. It emerged that the television and, in particular television commercials, had played an active role in John's early learning – he had known all the commercials by heart and would recite them as they appeared on the screen. His independent learning must have been supported by his ability to hypothesise about the relationship between language and print and to ask himself the right kinds of questions.

When Jane Torrey wrote her account of John's success in teaching himself to read, she was concerned to dispel the idea that working class children were less likely to be successful learners than middle class children (especially if they had no one to help them). Until recently it was assumed that children who grew up in homes that were not 'bookish' were at a disadvantage in school. As it became clearer that children could learn to read a great deal about reading independently, it was no longer possible to generalise about what parents *have* to do to help their children to become successful readers.

For a long time schools were undecided about involving parents in their reading programmes. Sometimes this was because teachers were defensive of their professional status. At this time, in the nineteen sixties and seventies, many educationalists believed that education had to compensate for children's home backgrounds; this way of thinking reinforced the notion that learning began at school. Even a decade ago the idea of a partnership between home and school was not far advanced.

Home-school reading programmes

During this period some important projects were, however, set up to promote parental participation, the most notable of which was undoubtedly the Haringey Reading Project (Tizard, Schofield and Hewison 1982). The response to this project was remarkable and parents in the project schools became involved almost without exception. The key feature of the project was that parents of top infant children in two classes from different schools heard them read at home on a regular basis, from books chosen by the class teachers. The children's subsequent progress in reading was compared with that of a control group who had no extra help of this kind. At the end of a two year research period, when comparisons were made, it was realised that children who had received regular support from parents were substantially ahead of their peers in the control group. This included

children who read to parents who could not themselves read English. It was findings like this that prompted the development of similar projects, such as the Belfield Reading Project (Jackson and Hannon 1981) and an initiative undertaken by the Coventry Community Education Project (Widlake and MacLeod 1984). In some parts of the country, though, pockets of resistance to the very idea of involving parents still remained.

So during the sixties and early seventies the main message to parents had been to leave the teaching of reading to the professionals. The late seventies and early eighties had seen the introduction of projects which proved that parents *were* interested and, when invited, would participate in schools' reading programmes and make an important contribution. Yet even where the pattern had changed to involve parents, professionals still told parents what to do and involvement was limited.

The largest and probably the most long-lasting initiative of this kind was developed in ILEA. It was called PACT (parents, children and teachers). It grew out of the work of the Pitfield Project, set up in 1979, and offered a variety of support to promote home-school reading programmes. Materials were developed for schools to use, including video programmes and suggested formats for written dia-logues with parents about children's reading experiences at home and at school.

A PACT scheme is most effective when the school works alongside the parents and is aware of children's linguistic and cultural backgrounds, so that the shared reading experiences are meaningful and enjoyable. The following example of a PACT scheme comes from a school where the practice of working with parents has been well-established for a number of years. Elizabeth Dawson, an infant teacher, describes the background to school policy, and provides an example from a written dialogue between herself and a child's mother.

From the beginning of their school career, children are encouraged to read a wide variety of books, and to take them home to read with their parents. The accompanying booklet is a way of fostering home-school links, and encouraging parents and children to realise that we value 'home' experiences. I have also sometimes used the booklet to open discussion about another matter – e.g. a change in the child's behaviour – with a parent. Conversely, some parents have used the booklet to raise particular concerns with me.

Every week, I try always to write something about how the child has read and/or responded to the book with me, and then to suggest a way to read the book at home (talk about the pictures, point to the words, read the book aloud together, etc.), according to the child's stage of development. Particularly in the early stages, a child may well be taking books home which s/he cannot read independently, so it is important to suggest to parents how they might use the book, and to make it clear that it is not appropriate to expect the child to read the text without help! Specific skills and strategies can also be suggested: for example, if the child is reluctant to make guesses at words s/he doesn't know, I ask the parent to encourage 'sensible' guessing (and explain what I mean by this), and to praise the child's efforts even when the guess is 'wrong'.

We find the parental interest and involvement with their children's reading development does tend to tail off in the Juniors, as their children become independent and fluent readers. There are, however, some parents who con-tinue in written dialogue with the teachers right through the school. Of course, the tenor of the 'conversation' changes, and becomes more concerned with attitudes, critical responses, and developing tastes than with the actual mechanics of the reading process.

This example shows the scheme working at its best. When a parent like this one is able to write to me every week, a very valuable dialogue is established. These parents take up my suggestions about how to help C., and comment on how she responds at home. With their particular knowledge of their child, they have also enabled me to see when I haven't got it quite right for her, so that I modified my plans.

With this kind of encouragement from home and school, C. has developed the confidence to read and discuss fiction, non-fiction and poetry. Her parents have also reinforced specific features of the reading/writing system which I had pointed out to C. e.g. use of capital letters, speech marks and other punctuation. C. now uses these quite spontaneously – and usually accurately – in her own writing.

I find it an enormous encour-agement to work with parents in this way, and the benefits to the child have been obvious.

Elizabeth Dawson

In 1984 Griffiths and Hamilton reported on the PACT project in a book called, *Parent, Teacher, Child: Working Together in Children's Learning* and it became even clearer that, in schools where parents were invited to be partners with teachers, standards were raised and reading became something both worthwhile and pleasurable.

Cooperation between parents and teachers in children's learning is a comparatively new field, although the research findings and examples of good practice are accumulating. The one clear direction in which such co-operation does take us is away from the traditional split between home and school and towards a genuine sharing of responsibility for children's education. We believe that this could signal a real turning-point for children and their learning . . . Whatever the future holds, we are now convinced that parents must be included as partners in their children's learning.

(Griffiths and Hamilton, 1984)

Book	Tick if read	Date	Comments if wished
The sick cow		Teacher 23-1	This one's shorter—maybe it's also still the pictures that Carly needs. I'll try her on another longer book later
			on, but as you say, there's still a lot of mileage in shorter books + it would be awful if she got put off reading !
The sick Cow		Parent 29.1	Carly read this book twice, she read it very well, breaking up the words that she wasn't sure of. She was much happier reading this and read it quite quickly.
The Light-house Keeper's Catastrophe		Teacher 30-1	Quite a difficult book- but with pictures !! Carly tended to lose the thread a bit so still needs a bit of support
		Parent 5.2.	Carly read this book over a couple of days. She read it very well and the pictures helped her not to lose interest.
The Bears of Hemlock Mountain		Teacher 6 - 2	Carly opted for this book, and seemed really interested in it. She summarized the first 2 chapters for me and I think will be able to enjoy + persist with this.
		Parent 11.2	Carly enjoyed this book as the chapters weren't too long. She read 5 chapters on her own. I just helped her with words that she wasn't sure of.
The Most Wonderful Egg in the World		Teacher 13 - 2	Carly told me some of the story from "The Bears of Hemlock Mountain" + seems to have enjoyed it. This one is easier + shorter again. She read most of it fluently
		Parent	Carly skipped through this book and enjoyed it
			She liked the pictures. Carly is now reading on her own.

The term 'partnership' implies a two-way collaborative process but in many home and school schemes there has been a tendency for the school to determine the nature of the initiative, This has sometimes resulted in neglect of the fact that reading (and writing) are social activities which depend very much on the expectations that parents and children have about literacy, both in school but also in their lives outside school. Recent work on literacy has looked more closely at the social contexts in which children learn about reading and writing.

Literacy at home

Ethnographic studies such as the one carried out by Shirley Brice Heath in *Ways With Words* (1983) offered an insight into the oral and literacy traditions of different communities in the Piedmont Carolinas of the USA, and helped to show that reading and writing play important roles both in representing social beliefs and practices and in empowering individuals.

One British study influenced by the work of Shirley Brice Heath was carried out by Hilary Minns. This study involved investigating a number of four-year-old children's literacy experiences at home prior to their starting school. The children in the study were carefully chosen to represent the intake in this Coventry school both in social, cultural and linguistic terms. As the head teacher of the school, Hilary Minns felt strongly that if she wanted to learn more about the children and their reading she needed to go out into the community and to find out more about their respective families' interests in language and literacy. It was a salutory experience for her, as she found she had underestimated both the nature and the range of literacy-related activities with which the children and their families were already engaging. Her book *Read It To Me Now* (1990) grew out of this study of five young children and their families: one Afro-Caribbean child, two Asian, and two white children – two girls and three boys.

Minns points us in the right direction when she describes the way forward for home and school links:

In order to become conscious of pre-school experiences and their differences and to add a social dimension to our knowledge of the reading process, we need to give ourselves a new way of looking at what children might be doing when they come to school . . . At present we know little about the knowledge of reading they bring to school . . . and still less about what parents might have done to help . . . in spite of their involvement in home-school reading projects. Our knowledge of the cultural beliefs and values of families and their effect on children as readers has to be made a professional concern.

Hilary Minns believes that there is a long way to go before schools and parents are working together – not merely in a superficial contractual sense but so that a two-way understanding is at the heart of planning and practice.

In another study, David Roll, a teacher in a junior school in south-east London, has also tried to understand more fully the expectations that the parents of the bilingual children in his class had of the school. In an unpublished dissertation, *What Language Shall we Talk Today* (1988) he examined the literate lives of four eight-year-old children in the context of their homes. Of the four families represented, one family had roots in India but had lived for some years in East Africa, one originated from the Pakistani border of the Punjab, and two came from the Punjab. The first family spoke Hindi and Swahili as well as English, while the languages of the other three families included Urdu, Panjabi, and classical Arabic. Religion played an important part in these families' lives, and the Hindu, Sikh and Moslem faiths were represented in the families studied.

Shirley Brice Heath's approach in *Ways With Words* sought to define the elements in a community's literacy practices. Roll focused on the variations and differences in the lives and attitudes of the Asian families he interviewed. He invited the families to talk about their views of how their children became linguistically competent (in spoken and written languages) at home and at school, and how they felt mother tongue maintenance should be encouraged and developed in both contexts. Although there were many common factors it became quite clear that there were also differences, and that these influenced how parents perceived both their own role and the role of the school.

In Roll's concluding comments he had these things to say about what needs to be taken into account *before* establishing school policy:

Children's particular experiences of literacy

The notion of pre-school literacy as an homogenous activity is a fallacy. Particularly in the first few years of schooling then, full account must be taken of variations in such experiences. As one result of my research, I would suggest that the only way in which such variations can continually be given adequate consideration is through the analysis of children in their literacy contexts at the micro, rather than the macro, level.

Learning from parents

Whilst the school has been shown to value home experiences and has spent a considerable time liaising with parents, it is debatable how effective these efforts have been. There is little doubt that to explain the school's approach to literacy to the local community is a valuable activity, yet there is a distinct danger that this can become merely a one way process, with teachers imparting their knowledge to the supposed needy.

Studies such as those undertaken by Minns and Roll indicate that there is much work still to be carried out to create an approach to children's literacy development at home and at school that is based upon agreed ways of working.

The *Primary Language Record* (1988), which at the time of Roll's study was in an embryonic stage but is now well established, can contribute a great deal to this shared understanding of literacy. The *Record* provides a framework for documenting a child's progress and development between the ages of three and eleven and a substantial part of the record-keeping is devoted to the contributions and views of the parents (and the child). Part A of the record establishes a powerful forum, an opportunity for parents to be informants and for teachers to be aware of the range of reading opportunities with which children engage.

This range can include TV, video, computers and print in the home,

The Primary Language Record

community and school. Children may be reading and writing story, poetry and information texts as well as letters, lists, and other kinds of texts in use in their homes. In addition they may be meeting a range of symbol systems and scripts. All these 'literacy events' and more can play an influential part in any child's development, particularly in contexts where children are led to make links between their past experiences and the new learning that they meet.

In the following example from the *Primary Language Record* we learn a great deal about one child's range of learning experiences and the connections between different aspects of his developing literacy. N. is six years old (Year 1) and is a monolingual English-speaking child. The extracts from his record are taken from discussions between N's mother and the class teacher.

Part A To be completed during the Autumn Term

A1 Record of discussion between child's parent(s) and class teacher *(Handbook pages 12-13)*

N. enjoys sharing the P.A.C.T books with his mum and other relatives. He still has a set of favourite books which he likes to return to again and again. He regularly visits the library, which he enjoys. He is still interested in using his computer and typing in words. He often adds his own captions to drawings he does at home. He enjoys making birthday cards for relatives. He still likes watching cartoons on T.V. He notices print in the environment - eg street signs, names on food packets etc. Enjoys puzzles and playing with his friends. A bedtime story is a must - enjoyed by N. and his mum. He still talks

Signed Parent(s) .... Teacher ....

non-stop at home to relatives and friends.

Date ....

A2 Record of language/literacy conference with child *(Handbook pages 14-15)*

A1 Record of discussion between child's parent(s) and class teacher

This example is packed with information and there is plenty of evidence here that N. takes part in a wide range of literacy-related activities outside school; nine are referred to within this record. His experiences of written language are described like this:

Enjoys sharing PACT books with his mum and other relatives

still has a set of favourites which he like to return to again and again

he regularly visits the library which he enjoys

continued interest in computers – uses it to type words

often adds captions to drawings at home

enjoys making birthday cards

still likes watching cartoons on TV

notices print . . . street signs, names of food

a bedtime story is a must – enjoyed by N. and his mum

Information like this contributes to the teacher's understanding of the child and helps her teaching plans.

Two other points in this discussion are worth noting. One is the role that this boy's mother plays in supporting his learning at home, and the importance of other relatives in his family, who are mentioned in several places in the record as taking part in his literacy activities. The other point concerns the affective aspect of his learning. Almost every literacy experience referred to in the discussion is introduced by expressions such as "enjoys", "likes to return to", "continued interest in", "still likes", and so on. Observations like these indicate Neil's commitment to and pleasure in his learning, and the importance of this to his continuing progress.

The *Primary Language Record* has provided a meeting point for parents and teachers and has often led to improved relations between home and school. Because the discussion with parents generally takes place in the autumn term, the contact established in this way, early in the school year, has often led to further communication later in the year. Where parents can participate more fully in the life of the school and where schools invite this participation, even closer understandings can be established. We invited a parent from a school where the *Primary Language Record* is in use to describe her initial reactions to her children's primary school experiences and how her views have changed with time. The parent quoted here is a Turkish and English speaking mother of two children aged four and eight, who attended the same school. At first she was not sure what was happening:

Where I come from the education system is totally different. I used to think what are they doing? Why are these children sitting on the carpet? Why aren't they copying what's written, from the blackboard?

But in time with more experience of the classroom, she came to see that learning was going on:

I realised that they are learning much better like this. By sitting with other children sharing, they are learning when they are copying each other or just watching or helping each other. Because they do help each other a lot.

She indicated that her views about reading had shifted too, in response to the practice she had observed in the school:

They used to read by heart. I thought it wrong when it wasn't. I started coming into school and saw other children doing the same thing, where I think it's normal now. There's nothing wrong with that – that's the way they learn.

She appreciated the school's interest in her children's bilingualism and was supporting their development in Turkish at home:

At home we read and we always talk in Turkish. We get videos and I have a lot of books. I try to encourage them, not forcing them. I tell them it's nice to know as many languages as you can, because it's an advantage.

They're both bilingual, English and Turkish equal.

Parents have appreciated being more closely involved in their children's education through the *Primary Language Record*. A father said he felt for the first time he had not merely been consulted about his child's education at school but had actually contributed to it. When a real dialogue of this kind begins between teachers and parents, children must benefit.

One mother who had been concerned about her child's apparent lack of confidence as a reader at home was taken aback when she visited the school for her first *Primary Language Record* discussion with the class teacher. The teacher assured her that her son was really enjoying books, and showed her his language and literacy conference, which had been completed a week earlier. The mother was amazed to read:

Matthew loves reading and has 'thousands' of books at home, mostly on his shelves in his bedroom. Prefers to read by himself in his bedroom. Really enjoys the Narnia series. His father read all the series to him.

The mother said that it had been "brilliant" to read the first words in this conference: "Matthew loves reading." She admitted : "We thought he didn't! As a result I was made to feel more positive about his reading – he shot ahead that year." He began to talk more about his school experiences at home, and to take things into school, which he had never done before. Being able to discuss his own progress with the teacher, and knowing that his parents had been communicating with his teacher, had made all the difference to his view of himself as a reader.

Some of the latest examples in this chapter have related to bilingual parents and children. The need that schools have felt to establish contact with bilingual children's families, and to find out more about the language, and literacy experiences of children with whom teachers may not share a language has often provided the impetus for schools to make better home-school links. But many schools, including those where all the children speak only English, frequently find there is a gap that needs to be bridged between the cultural and educational assumptions of teachers and those of the parents of the children they teach. Often, obvious linguistic and cultural difference simply highlights a question that needs to be faced anyway.

All schools need to recognise that their ideas about how reading development is best encouraged may not coincide with the views of their parents, and be ready to establish a continuing dialogue between parents and teachers on this subject. Teachers need to know about the home literacy experiences that are the foundation of school learning. Similarly, parents can support their children more effectively if they have a clear understanding of the school's approach. As teachers we can learn from a working relationship with parents that fosters trust and respect.

When we look back at the history of relations between homes and schools we can see that a number of significant changes have taken place over the last two or three decades. At the beginning of the period there was a tendency to discourage parental involvement in the learning and teaching of reading. The nineteen seventies saw a marked shift away from this position, and a number of projects were set up to encourage home-school reading schemes, but these tended to emphasise school views of literacy teaching and ignore learning and reading experiences outside school. Over the last few years there has been a more towards more equal relationships, with all partners in the reading process working together.

Above all, our improved knowledge of development, both before children start school and during their school years, has taught us not to assume that any child comes to school with a 'literacy deficit'. Rather, each child arrives with different experiences and understandings, and these must form the basis of their continuing learning.

A continuing dialogue

A day in the life of a reader

SUSAN

(Year 2; languages: English, parents speak Twi at home)

Alyson Russen made written observations of a child in her class during one day at school from first thing in the morning until the middle of the afternoon. Until recently Alyson had observed that Susan was very much lacking in confidence at school. Making these notes consolidated her impressions of Susan's developing confidence in her approach to reading and writing, and of how her peers are playing a major part in this development.

9.15

During registration Susan's eyes showed that she was trying to read the Daychart (information on what's happening and general points about work tasks and groups). I asked her to read out a few lines at the top of the chart which are mostly the same every day, and she did so.

9.30

Sharing news session. Susan had been to a Ronald McDonald party with some cousins and showed a bag of goodies which included a plastic glove puppet. At home she had written on a scrap of paper some talk for the puppet along the lines of "Hello, how are you?" etc. which she read out to us introducing it as a 'show'. There had been a lot of wriggling and hissing during register which I suspect was Susan trying to stop her neighbours from seeing her writing.

10.00

Susan was teaching two children to play a shape recognition game which she and a group of children had made. She was very confident, electing herself as the person to read out the cards and therefore to control the game. Her voice and manner were very strong and assured, not only were the descriptions that she has to read well known to her, the answers were too.

11.30

I suggested Susan do some writing in her 'Think Diary' and then asked her if she would like to choose a book for our Favourite Book Table (they stick a post-it note on the front saying why they chose it). Susan chopped and changed endlessly, reading other people's choices and I think being influenced by them, finding it hard to settle on one book. She eventually chose *Not Now Bernard* (David McKee) and wrote "I like this book this is my best book because its cool". When I asked her, she said that she didn't think it was cool, she chose it because she remembered it from long ago, but that she had learnt the word 'cool' from her brother and wanted to use it.

12.00

Went straight from the above to reading time. Susan and a friend were looking at a finger rhyme book and were then joined by Mary-Ann. She could read all the rhymes, so she read and Susan did the finger movements copying those from the book and joining in with the rhyme's choruses. A lot of laughing and ad libbing the rhymes.

1.30

After wet play Susan came and showed me a letter that Mary-Ann had written on the typewriter during playtime. Susan was extremely impressed with this achievement, read the letter to me and asked Mary-Ann if she could keep it.

2.15

Susan had been drawing a sheep's skull and vertebrae and labelling them. She was very interested and absorbed. When she finished I asked her if she would like to look at an information book on bones with me. She found a page showing different skulls and matched them to our wallchart on skeletons. She commented on the smallness of the writing (small = difficult for Susan) and asked me to read two passages for her. She showed the book to others who were doing the same activity but told them they'd have to ask me if they wanted it read.

Teachers talking about teaching

'It is a prerequisite of successful teaching of reading, especially in the early stages, that whenever techniques are taught, or books are chosen for children's use, meaning should always be in the foreground'.

English for ages 5-16

Teachers talking about teaching

The teacher's role is complex. Much of what it is that successful teachers actually do has yet to be documented; there is a great deal of pedagogical theory in education, but much less actual documentation of the multiple interactions between teachers and learners that support children's progress. In the chapter that follows, we look at the role of the teacher in the teaching and learning of reading, and try to define what makes for effective practice in this area.

Teaching reading is a "practical art"; teachers develop their practice by *doing* it. This can make it difficult for them to communicate what they do, and to define what it is in what they do that makes the difference. We have therefore chosen to approach this subject by juxtaposing two interviews with experienced primary teachers. Margaret Wyeth is a deputy head teacher and Gill Verde is a language coordinator in the London Borough of Greenwich. The schools they teach in are culturally mixed and multilingual. Between them they have forty years experience of teaching and of teaching reading; both have taught in junior and infant departments. Moreover, both have been at their present schools for a number of years, and therefore have experience of developing common understandings and formulating common approaches with their colleagues over an extended period. Both have contributed to many in-service courses, and are used to describing their practice to others. As will become apparent, both have some key experiences in common.

Through these interviews we hope to be in a better position to define how teachers teach, and what they know. As they reflect on the changes that they have seen take place over their years of teaching, they help us to see the developments in the teaching of reading in terms of their own stories.

Margaret Wyeth talks to Anne Thomas

I thought you might like to talk about the ways in which your views about teaching and learning of reading have developed over the last few years?

If I go back to fourteen or fifteen years to when I was a junior teacher, I think that it was then that I suddenly thought there must be more to reading than *Wide Range Readers* and this boring reading scheme called *Royal Road*. That's what we had all those years ago in the junior school, that was it. If you were an O.K. reader or fairly fluent you were given *Wide Range*, and if you were struggling you were immediately put on to *Royal Road*. We were a separate infant and junior school; the infant school taught children on *Reading with Rhythm*. Then they came into the junior school and were immediately taken off any form of *Reading with Rhythm*, there weren't even any *Reading with Rhythm* books there. And then we would say, let's see how well you can read?

What was it about 'Royal Road Readers' that the school felt was important for children at seven plus who were having difficulties?

The *Royal Road Readers* scheme as far as I could understand was given because it was a phonic-based scheme. There were no real stories in these things, just odd words and they had to learn them. Then they learnt sentences, and then they moved on to rather awkward books like *Jim Sands and the Bandit*, that was one of the books I remember. But with *Wide Range Readers*, if you could read, you were all put on *Blue Book One*, If I thought you were quite good, I still wouldn't have given you *Book Two* – this is how I understood reading to be, everyone started on the same book.

There were accompanying comprehension exercises to go with the book, and you didn't move on to the next book until you had completed the comprehension exercises. I had a very bright child in my class, aged eight, whose mother was concerned that he was reading at a very low level at school, which he was. I remember saying to her, well you know it's our policy, they have to have done all the comprehension exercises before they can move on to the next book. At eight this child was more than fluent, he probably could have read Tolkein and enjoyed it, but he was kept on 'Wide Range' Book Two or whatever. Meanwhile the children on *Royal Roads* were withdrawn from the class, and so you got the 'jumper brigade' forming because as they got older and were still on *Royal Road* everybody knew why these children were being taken out, and they would attempt to hide the book and put it up the jumper. It was dreadful really.

And you obviously questioned . . .

Well I thought – anybody could teach reading like this, I mean you haven't got to be a teacher. I thought there must be more to it than this, there's something radically wrong here. The children on *Royal Road* who were struggling still struggled, and they hated books, not surprisingly. The third and fourth year junior children who had gone through all the *Wide Range Readers* were then termed 'free readers' and were never really taught to read after that, you just forgot them. I mean they read, but only if they wanted to. Every child was heard to read but it wasn't reading *with* a teacher, there was no partnership about it, it was "Come and read to me", and they read a page. Then the rest of the time it was very much regarded as something you went and did when you'd finished your work. "You go and read and keep out of my hair" sort of thing.

I recognise it all.

So that's how it was, and then I remember going on a course at CLPE. This is going back to 1979 or so, when they had six week courses, and it was a reading and writing course. I learned different things to try out, for instance reading the text to the child first, can they read it back? Tape them reading and retelling a well known story – how near to the text were they able to get? Getting them to predict, you know, reading in small groups and then predicting what you think is going to happen next? It was interesting because the children who you thought "Oh yes, they can read", sometimes hadn't got a clue what they were reading about.

When I came back from the course we did branch out and buy more books, but it was difficult because I wasn't the language postholder. So we bought a lot more scheme books, as well. They were all colour-coded, but even then it provided the children with a wider reading choice. I think that they were used still as a straight-jacket though, because you found teachers saying "No you can't read that book, it's not the colour band that you are on". I would like to say also that some of those *Wide Range Readers* were alright, there was nothing wrong with some of those stories, it was just the whole school organisation.

And, as you say, the way in which the children's choice was constrained.

Yes, and so I think your views on reading develop within the school you're in. You've got to make gentle shifts. You can make shifts within yourself, but as a school it takes a lot longer, because people must see for themselves what needs to be done and believe in it so that they will do it well.

How I see reading now has a great deal to do with enabling children to feel confident as readers. I think they need to feel good about themselves, and feel successful, and not feel frustrated. They need time to look through a book and get familiar with it, as well as time to read with the teacher. We have to bear in mind that not all children are going to grow up to be avid readers, just as they will not all grow up to have a great love of art, or writing, or sport. But it's our job to teach them skills and help them see the purpose of learning to read. All this applies to juniors too – monitoring and conferencing shouldn't be something that's only done whilst they're learning the mechanics.

That idea of the 'free reader' from years ago, just wasn't on, was it, because children continue to learn to read throughout their school lives.

Yes, though there is sometimes still this feeling of 'OK they can read, I'm not going to worry about them'. But there is much more to it than that. I remember a teacher here was once conferencing with a child in the third year juniors; he was a child who was struggling with reading but he felt he had done quite well. And the teacher said

"Well what was it, why do you feel that you are making better progress this year?" and he said to her "It's because you read the book to me first". These are the sort of strategies you automatically use with infants, you sit and read the book through so that they know what the stories are and they start to learn. But as they get older there will still be children in the class that need to have the book read through first, and I think sometimes that's not always done.

I've seen that happen in secondary schools as well, where children are virtually not read to at all, and those that still can't read have got no models. So yes, I'm sure you're right.

It's important to avoid putting children on the spot, and making them unsure. One of our students was here the other day and a child was reading the book to her and doing *Lazy Mary, Lazy Mary*. We were only just getting to know it as a class, she was trying to take it on for the first time with an adult and I heard the student say "No, what is that word?" and I thought "I've got to stop this straight away" because I could see Marie was looking very puzzled. If a child experiences that every day, someone saying "No, that's not it, what is that?" – you'd give up in the end wouldn't you?

Yes you would, and you'd also have a very fixed idea about what reading is all about. I wonder if you could tell me something about the practical way you organise the reading now in your classroom. For instance, what about provision? I know it's an enormous area, but I just wondered if you could consider what you think are the key elements in your classroom, things that you wouldn't be without?

Well, first of all I think it's very, very important that you have a well organised book area. I wouldn't like to see my books just jumbled on a shelf, I think that it's nice to basket them up in some way. To start off with, with the reception class, I tend to have a basket of 'Books we know'. I read a book to them and when they know the story, it will go in the 'Books we know basket'. Obviously that gets choc-a-bloc within a week or two, so then we start to break them up. If it's a book that we think we know we can read fairly quickly, there's not a lot of words in it, we would put it in a basket called 'quick reads'. If it's got more words we put it in 'longer reads'. Then the children naturally start to group all the *Spot* books together, and I keep the *Story Chest* books together, because it's quick. I mean you've got to just know your way round the book area and so have the children, It's very daunting isn't it, if you're a five year old and you come in and see a mass of books all put together any old how, you wouldn't know your way round it. So I think you've got to have a very well organised book area,

There are certain books that I wouldn't not like to be without. When I was looking at them I found they were nearly all books that have got a rhythm. It was *Each Peach Pear Plum* and others like that, because you notice that children just naturally take on that singing rhythm.

I wouldn't be without having an alphabet in my room and that's something else we sing through. The other day a child asked me "What does a Y look like?" I asked her if she knew her alphabet – and she said "Yes", so I asked her to sing through the alphabet and stop when she got to Y. We've got alphabets there in the writing area, and one up on the wall, and then there are masses of them in the book area.

I wouldn't be without Big Books as well. I think it's just lovely watching children share a Big Book with a friend. They sit there and point along the words and read it together and talk about it. Big Books are fairly new aren't they? I mean it's only in the last four or five years that we've had them in this school. Also, I think it's important you have an 'information basket' basket of books, and that goes for the whole school. We have a little basket with a collection of poetry books too, and then those music books, the ones I play the guitar from. I leave them there and the children sit there and sing through them, and of course they see the musical notations, and start to make their own little music books.

Obviously the baskets of books have names and first thing in the morning when they come in I have the collection of baskets there and they come straight in and sit and read. I always make sure I have the 'Books we've made' basket out and the 'Information books' basket out as well as the '*Spot* books' and the 'Quick Reads' and '*Story Chests*'.

So how long would you spend first thing in the morning?

Usually they come in at nine and we usually go on to about twenty or twenty-five minutes past which is a good span for fairly young children. But I think it's because they read with a friend. They will go and get a Big Book and sit with a group of friends reading it through. It's a time for them to practise what they know about reading, as well as reread favourite books.

At drink-time every day I always read three books to them. I read them a book that they know very well and one that I've read to them before, and then I read them a new book. One they know very well, one they know quite well and then a new one, so they get to learn the books.

It's difficult to separate what you've just been talking about from the next bit, but the next bit is important. The notion of inviting children to learn to read 'real books', is thought by some to be a method of teaching, a not-very-structured approach in which children learn to read by osmosis – or some of them do, and the rest of them fall by the wayside. What I would like you to talk about is what you actually do in the way of supporting children and what kind of strategies you use to help them gain access to print.

First of all, in each infant class there are 40 books that are the same, so that as the children move from class to class they immediately feel familiar with some of the books that are on offer in that classroom. I'm not saying that every classroom has got exactly the same number of books but all of them have got these forty books that we think are brill. You could go into any room and find *Not Now Bernard*. I think it is very important that the children don't go from this classroom into another classroom and think 'Gosh, I don't know any of these books'.

Some of these books are available as big books as well, and I think that children learn a lot about reading from our shared reading sessions. They learn all kinds of things to do with reading, the direction of the print, the way the text is laid out – in a song, for instance – and the way the words are written. They can practise what they know about reading and join in the reading. I find that children quite often begin to focus on the print in these shared reading sessions, and point out the letters in their name, the sounds words begin with, and so on. Sometimes when we're reading a Big Book I will cover up a word with a 'flap', and encourage them to predict what it says, and then check their predictions.

We also do quite a lot of shared writing in this class, sometimes in small groups and sometimes in the larger group. That's where children begin to learn a great deal about reading, by seeing words written down in front of them, and actually sharing in the writing. Obviously we decide together what to write, but sometimes children will begin to tell me how to write a particular word, too, if they know how it begins, or if it is like other words they're familiar with. I'm often surprised to find out how much children know about language in these sessions. They'll often point out punctuation, too, and tell me where to put a full stop, or they'll ask me to write a word like BOOM in big letters.

Like 'Meg and Mog'?

Yes, and like comics. We do also play with words quite a bit and look at their shapes and have fun with their sounds. This follows on quite naturally from the singing that we do. The children know a lot of traditional rhymes, and we make collections of those in books for them to read together, and sometimes we make up our own rhymes and songs and talk about how to make them rhyme. Children do become aware of the patterns of language in this kind of way, and begin to put two and two together when they come to write. It's really through their own writing that you start to see from quite early on what it is that they are noticing in their reading.

With older children I would spend more time looking at words they know and at how they're spelled, making lists of words in families, lists of words that sound the same, lists of words that look the same, and so on. I'd be keeping a class word bank for children to add to, and I'd be encouraging them to find the small words they know inside longer words. I'd get them to look at beginnings and endings and see how they are put together. There are some books that really help children see that – like *My Cat Likes to Hide in Boxes*.

I've got children in my class now who are learning to read quite a few books. I mean, you could sit alongside them and they would read with you, and if you do a running record they'd be quite accurate with a lot of them, and yet would I say they were readers? No I wouldn't say they were fully fledged readers. . . but they have learnt a lot about reading. And then gradually they take on more of the process with books that they know. They move from chanting 'Sing, sing, sing-a-song' to sweeping their finger along the line. And then they start to actually focus in on each word as they read. When you see children self correcting, when they start to go back and reread passages, then you know that they are beginning to grasp it and are really taking on reading. And when you're carrying out a running record and they insert a word that is a meaningful substitute, you know that they are grasping it. We were talking about the child who constantly picks what looks like an easy read and we were saying, is that a problem? I think that you just monitor that child's choice of books and then say, "So you like books about bears do you? Well how about reading . . .?

So, as far as their actual strategies are concerned, you think that once they start to self correct they make an enormous leap in their development and they are really begin to focus on the print. And you also notice children going back and beginning to read particular passages. Are there any other strategies that you help them develop?

Yes. For instance, if they were looking at the word 'picture' and they hadn't got it, I would probably say to them "Okay what does the word begin with?" and they would say "P" and get the initial sound of it and I would then say "Is it a long word or a short word?" and encourage them to have a go at sounding out some of the letters in it, But if they didn't get it, I wouldn't make a great big thing about it. I'd either tell them or they would probably substitute something else if they were confident. I think it's only when they are not confident with you that they say "I don't know that".

So though the story is an important part of learning to read...

Yes, so is sounding out some of the words. We are not saying that sounding out is something that was done twenty years ago and is never to be done again. Nobody is throwing out any of the good things at all, are they?

No, they are just helping children have a widest range of strategies as possible. Sometimes we need to be concerned about children round about the age of six or seven who are thoroughly enjoying books, but for some reason don't understand that we need eventually to be accurate in our reading. I'm wondering what approach you take then?

Well if I found that they were being totally inaccurate in their reading but loving having a go at it all, I would say "Now come on, let's look more closely at this", because I do think they have to be told. It's like their writing, when they are having a go with spelling, if you let them think that 'like' is l, k, i, e, forever and a day, well it's not going to be good enough. You can't have a child go on thinking any old thing will do.

Yes, I think that's right and I think it is important to say that. Is there anything else we need to say about helping children on their way to becoming confident readers?

I think basically speaking, by the time the child has been in school for about a year, a full school year, you have got a fair idea if they are coping and progressing well, so we are talking about age six. At six you have got a very good idea, and if they are not, then you need to start assessing how that child feels about themselves as a reader, and looking closely at them. I am thinking of a child that I had last year who isn't operating very well for his age and yet if you look at how he started in the nursery, and his *Primary Language Record* from that time, he has made phenomenal progress but there is still a cause for concern.

I think if you are worried about a child there are lots of things that you can do. Maybe just talking with them and finding out if they have a favourite book for a start. It's important to look for the sort of parental support that they have been receiving, or not as the case may be. It could well be due to some sort of pressure at home that the child is not taking on reading. You need to keep in close contact with the parents and find out their view and their concerns.

Children love to make their own little books and they like to learn to read these back, and I would encourage a child to keep doing that, whether they were six or nine or ten. They need to spend lots of time telling you stories and seeing you acting as scribe writing it down, and then having a go themselves. These are all ways I would deal with a child who was experiencing difficulty.

You can find a lot out by the way they are tackling the books, whether they are a little bit hesitant about coming and reading with you, whether they don't really know if they've got a favourite book, whether when you say "Come and read with me" they put down the book that they have been reading and go and get a 'reading' book. These things enable you to see the sort of experiences they've had.

And the view they have of reading.

Yes, and once you can understand that I think you can work out ways to extend it. For instance, if a child has got a hang-up about the text, then get some books that haven't got any words, or say "O.K., just tell a story to go with the pictures". Children at five are doing that all the time, and are encouraged to do it. Maybe this child has never experienced it. Then you can say, "Well that was your story with the picture, now I will read you the story that the person who made the book wrote and let's see who's got the best story". I would use all those sorts of strategies. Because the children might have had bad experiences.

Now, I always find these generalisations difficult, but I think we do know for a fact that there are many more boys than girls who for a number of reasons don't find learning to read something that they really want to achieve. Do you find that you've had boys like that in any of the classes of young children that we have talked about, and do you have any strategies to deal with it?

I have to honestly say that I have not had any five or six year old boys that have shown those signs, although they may have felt them. Certainly as they get older, they can often say "I don't like reading books". But I've found that if you always have information books available for children, that can be a real support. With some third-year junior children I had, we used to regularly go down to the public library and they were keen on dogs. None of them were really avid readers, but they got these books out on dogs and it was like a lift-off.

I found that having comics and magazines in the classroom was important, and the *Guinness Book of Records*, books that can be dipped into, books that don't have to be read from cover to cover. And books of instructions for making models – they do a lot of reading without realising it sometimes. Making class books is very important too, where you make your own information books. I was reading an information book about owls once, and the children were telling me some of the things they knew, and I thought right, next week we will make up our own little information book about owls. You don't have to read novels to be called a reader do you? I don't think it's right that boys and girls feel that the only way in is through stories.

Yes, so children have a view that reading involves an enormous number of things, including reading in more than one language, of course. How do you support the reading development of the bilingual children in the class?

Well one teacher in the school, Mr. Singh, is a Panjabi speaker and he can also read Urdu, so he works alongside me and supports children. And simultaneously, with a child like F. I sit and read books with her in English, and then she tries joining in with me, and she is gradually getting the rhythm of the language. I listen to her read and she's taking on that reading voice, do you know what I mean?

Yes, yes I do.

I wouldn't want people to think that "Oh you're alright, because you've got someone who can speak Panjabi or Urdu, but we haven't so we can't do anything for the child", because you can do a lot can't you, and other children can as well. If you've got two or three copies of a book in a first language they can all sit round together and join in and take it on. Parents can make tapes in children's home languages and write stories out. If Mr. Singh wasn't here then I'm sure G's mother would probably write out stories for us that we can use.

Are there other ways in which you work with parents, do they play a crucial role in supporting their childrens reading?

I think keeping the parents involved is absolutely vital. We have a meeting with them, with the parents in the nursery, and talk about books and the ways that the children are encouraged to read in the nursery. Then we have another talk to the parents when they come in to reception class about the home/school reading scheme, and the reading record book where we ask them to write down comments. That book goes from reception right through to fourth-year juniors. It is really fascinating to see how a child's parent has commented in the reception year and the different types of comments they are making by third- or fourth-year juniors. We explain about that and we show examples of the books. It's very important I think that you form a partnership with parents so they don't feel it's 'them and us', but that we are doing it together. And we talk generally about how we teach reading if you like, hopefully, not in a high-handed way because there's nothing worse.

We were talking about how your views have changed over the last few years, in thinking about the teaching of reading – where you've moved from, and where you think you are now.

I was always really interested in getting children to enjoy books – right from the start when we walked out of college. But I didn't really succeed very well . . .

You didn't succeed initially, you mean?

No, because of course we were on the old reading schemes. I came in to my first classroom, and it had a rather tatty book area. I can remember taking the books home and covering them and drawing pictures on the covers. But it didn't occur to me that the actual content of the book might need to be exciting. About a year or so after I started teaching, I took over the library and became interested in getting nice books for the library. That didn't really affect what the children could read before they went on to library book

So there were books to learn with, and then books to read.

Yes, that's right. I started to get a wider range of reading books as well. I understood that you needed attractive books for children to want to go and read them, but I still hadn't really begun to think about content – although I feel I should have done, because I was very interested in reading aloud to children. One of the ones I used to read in serial form was *Pinocchio*, and that was the book that they were all after. Really, if my brain cells had been working, I think I should have twigged then, all those years ago. I was interested in reading aloud to children, and exciting them with books in that way. I began to look around for good, colourful, interesting reading scheme books. We went through *Ladybirds*. They were great. I thought that if children went through 1A, B and C up to twelve A, B and C they were sure to read – but of course it didn't work out that way.

Do you mean, you weren't getting the results you hoped?

No, because I still brought it all down to words and sounds – some learned to read despite all my efforts, and others just didn't read. I was taking second-, third- and fourth-year juniors during those years. I'd still got some nice books and a wide range of reading books.

When you say reading books, you mean 'readers'?

Yes, reading schemes. I was about to make a new order of *Wide Range* and I looked at them and thought, "they bore

45

me silly and I'm going to find something else". So I found *Oxford Readers*, which were at least attractive but the stories were still pretty awful. Then I thought that Sheila McCullagh was the answer, but with still the same negative result really. Some children were readers and some were not – and some that could read chose not to.

At that point a new head arrived and suggested that I went into first-year juniors. These children didn't read and they didn't write, I asked them to write and they queued up. It was a tremendous culture shock for me. I had a friend who was doing a reading diploma who suggested I went to a reading conference at her college. And it suddenly was quite clear what was happening: there were all these wonderful books that I was putting into the library but I hadn't given them to the children.

What were they saying at that conference?

Look critically at your reading schemes: try reading them aloud and you'll find you can't. I came back to school and tried to read some of them aloud. I couldn't read them aloud to children, and yet I was expecting them to read them. That's when I began to look around. It was like a revelation really – something so obvious yet so new. Perhaps it was because I had been searching for an alternative that it clicked. I realised that the John Burningham books I'd been buying for my daughter could actually be the way in to reading for the children in my class. It was just like a bolt from the blue, and it was so obvious really.

So that's when I began to look around. I read Jill Bennett's *Learning to Read with Picture Books*, and I got a *Kaleidoscope* box in, and got all of Jill Bennett's recommendations. I kept *One, Two, Three and Away* beside these but I suppose I put more input into these new exciting books and *Story Chest*. By the middle of the year these more exciting books were being taken up. I read with them and there was a general buzz and enjoyment of books and it was really a revelation. The following year I taught children in the third and fourth years again. The headmaster said then that I could buy in the books that I wanted.

That was dramatic, wasn't it?

Well, I was so certain then. I remember coming back from that conference and getting the head in his room and saying "This is the way forward," and being very excited about it. I can remember him and the deputy saying "Oh it's great that someone is so enthusiastic", and saying "Alright let's see how it goes". . . There were other teachers in the school, too – one who was doing a reading diploma. She was obviously working along those lines as well and. . .

So that's important too, isn't it? – in terms of introducing a new way of working? That you've got people in there with a shared view?

Yes, I set up a really nice book corner, and I think that teachers began to see this and want other things too. We'd already gone through all the Cliff Moon stages, that had been going on before all this and we found it didn't work. It was an impossibility really – 13 stages.

How did you feel about the progress children were making in your class?

Well, they were reading in a very different way. They were reading for meaning – chunks of text. There was obvious enjoyment – wanting to read, and reading piles of books. There wasn't the sort of formality of reading one page or reading one chapter before going on. They would sit with piles of books on their desks and just really enjoy it – reading pages each. I suppose that's when I began to look at what they were doing through my record-keeping, and it just seemed so much better. During the next two years I did an Open University Language and Literacy course. That's when the book shop came in.

Yes, oh, tell me about that.

Well, the book shop was the result of this course. We had to do a big project – organising a book week or opening a book shop. It seemed to me that a book shop would be a good idea for our school, because it was pointed out that children who were readers before coming to school were book owners – they had favourite

books. So I put it to the staff. We've got no book shops in this area. The nearest one is in Woolwich, and the children's department is upstairs and out of the way. Our children generally don't get taken to book shops. They're not book owners and I doubt many of them are read to on a regular basis at home or even enough at school. So I thought, that's one way we could start to redress the balance. If we had a book shop in the school we'd at least give them the opportunity of being book owners. It worked in with a book event we were having, and we opened the book shop during that week. I had quite a long time to think about it, we were going to have it opened by one of the visitors who was coming in – and we had ribbons and balloons. . .

Brilliant! So it was an "event"?

It was an "event". I drew lots of Puffins on a leaflet and had them all photocopied and put 'Coming soon', and flooded the whole school with them. We got in a fine old state of excitement, and ordered about three hundred pounds worth of books. They did suggest five or six hundred but I thought three hundred was quite enough. . .

This is now from Books for Students?

Yes, they're our suppliers. We opened it with quite a loud bang on the Friday of the book week, and it just went on from there. . .

And that's gone on since that time?

Yes since that time. Every Friday. It must be six years now. The children put it out in the morning, so it's there for children to browse. In the afternoon the book shop is open. We have an auxiliary and a parent at the desk, and I have fourth-year children working in there tidying books, reading to children and ordering books. . .

This is in the hall?

In the top hall, yes, and classes are brought up there in turn. Sometimes two classes at a time. They can browse, buy, and reserve books. It's on a stamp system. Children can buy 50p, 20p or 10p stamps and they can save them if they want to.

So that means that most children have opportunities to buy. . .

All children have an opportunity to buy. Not all do, but we have a terrific turnover. We banked – in two weeks – three hundred pounds. We are a key account, second behind Roedean, no less! The children are very involved in the books.

I found that not only did our children become book owners, but it was also a way of finding out about newly published paperbacks, for us as staff as well. This is something that I didn't foresee. I would unpack books in the staff room, and they'd all be there looking at them and saying "Have you read this one" and "This is great". We'd buy the books. I mean things like. . . you know *Silly Stories* by Michael Rosen, what better book to make all children read! They'll read it again and again. And some of the poetry books go right through the school, because of the book shop. So it's a very important tool in our school, and a very important part of our school week. The top hall on Friday is our book shop base.

How did the success of the book shop affect your teaching?

Well, after two years with the fourth-year children, I was convinced that the books made an enormous difference to the children's success in reading. I still felt that some of my infant colleagues were thinking, "Yes, but she's not taught infants." I realised that it was quite true that I hadn't really tried this approach with children who had had little experience of reading. So that was when I asked to teach infants. I taught a middle-infant group. They had been in school one term, and some of them were in fact reception-age children. I had a really nice book area with lovely books and I threw out anything that I didn't quite approve of. I looked at these infants, who generally were non-readers and non-writers. How was I going to get them to have some sort of knowledge of these books? I went back to Don Holdaway at that point and discovered that in his reception class he had had about twenty books. That's how very slowly he introduced the books. I mean I had these three hundred or more books to introduce to my children!

That's something that people get confused by, really. It's not just the provision is it? It's how you use the provision.

I realised that this was really not good enough. Two things I focused on: first Don Holdaway's emphasis on reading aloud to children, getting them familiar with texts. And secondly Jeff Hynds' point about how successful those children who were book owners were. And of course they were also read to. I had thought that was probably quite important and I learnt that was one of the real keys to it. So I worked out a programme: I thought that when they came in in the morning we'd meet on the carpet and I would read to them. I followed Don Holdaway. I would read a familiar book, one that wasn't so familiar and a new one. Because our children generally were not read to, I felt that I needed to do a lot more reading to them. Then before lunch, at a quarter to twelve, I'd do the same thing.

Not the same three books?

Oh no, well, some of them might be – but it was always a familiar one, not such a familiar one and a new one. So I was gradually introducing more and more books. Then after lunch the children had access to those books I'd been reading to them, because we have a whole school policy of a 'silent' reading session (silent in inverted commas of course) from one until half past. . .

And that's a policy for the whole school?

Throughout the school, yes. Initially it would be five, ten minutes, and that grew until the children were sustaining their interest throughout the 25 to 30 minutes. And the end of that time they would come together on the carpet and they would read excerpts or poems or songs to me, and I would read back to them; or two of them would get together and read a page each – it was very much a sharing session. Then at the end of that I would do the same again – at least three books, familiar, not so familiar, and new. . .

So that's reading aloud three times a day, plus. . .

And the last half-hour of each day would always be a reading session anyway – storytime. Of course, it would be many more than three books at the last one because you'd have half an hour.

That's tremendous isn't it?

I didn't really know what to expect of infant children and what they were doing, I hadn't really sat back and observed them really well, so the *Primary Language Record* helped me in that, and Lynn Watkins (the IBIS Inspector) was very good at making me step back and watch what we were doing. At that point we worked out who was making progress – and virtually all of them were.

That's wonderful.

Yes, absolutely – it was incredible! I remember us coming down quite late from coffee once. They were all in the book corner and they were all involved in reading activities. We just stood at the door and watched them.

Tell me about S. and 'Just Like Daddy'.

She loved to read it, and very quickly wanted to read aloud to the children. If you remember I told you about them joining together. So she would share that with another child and she would read the *Just Like Daddy* bits rather than the more complicated text on every alternate page.

So that was an important strategy too, then?

Yes. They were very supportive to each other. . . she was another one who would just practise and practise and now she's reading fluently and writing at length.

In both languages?

Yes, S. is the only child who is truly biliterate. The others can speak two languages but not write them. There's a Panjabi session for all those who speak Panjabi once a week. It's only a half hour so it's not enough. There are books in community languages in this library, and we also have another little library where there are books in Panjabi and Urdu and Bengali. We have lots of languages within the school – at least seventeen. I think an appreciation of the different languages is as much as we really achieve, if I'm really honest; we do have the Panjabi classes but we very much feel as a staff that it's not enough, and not enough is made of it really. As I say, S. is the only one who is truly biliterate and her mother has done that.

Do you have some notion of where these children have got to now that they are second-year juniors? Tell me about that.

Well, they're all readers and all writers. People have mentioned they are quite an academic lot. But they are very ordinary children. Some of them. . . two of them in particular. . . come from families where the rest of the siblings have not been successful in school.

Could you just say something about their writing?

Well, I did notice that their writing was very much a reflection of the reading they had done. Book language was coming out in their writing, and that was quite astonishing to me. So we not only had these reading workshops but we were having writing workshops as well. They came regularly in to write after play in the morning and some of them just expanded almost overnight – they were able to write at length, and it was very exciting.

Tell me about the importance you think that favourite books have for children's development?

These children all liked stories and one boy, C., even though he knew very little English, loved *Witches Four*. That was his favourite book of all time. He used to read it over and over again – rehearsing it, and practising all the voices until he was satisfied. Then he would move on to another favourite. I think *Ahhh, said Stork* was probably the next one.

And these were all books that he'd heard you reading?

Oh yes, they were all in the classroom. The books also went home, the same books that I was introducing to them, and the ones that they had a go at reading, hard books as well, like *The Owl and the Pussycat*. Songs and rhymes I found were good fun. But what's so important for children if they are going to make sensible choices is for them to know what's inside the books. Older children conferencing and recommending books is quite a useful thing. Mine are very good at telling each other, "Have you read Peter Dickinson?" – that's an author they've recently found. And children introduce books to me as well. I remember them finding *The Elephant that Sat on Cars*, do you know that one by David Henry Wilson?

They like that. . .

It's so rude isn't it?!

It is possible from the evidence of these two teachers to identify common experiences they have had, to pinpoint particularly effective developments that took place in their respective schools, and to analyse their methods of working in the classroom.

The ways they thought about reading in the early stages of their careers were almost entirely influenced by the explicit policies in force in their schools. At this time, in the nineteen seventies, it was common practice for school reading policies to be determined by the particular reading scheme or schemes that were currently in use. This kind of policy could from today's standpoint be seen as deskilling teachers; the reading scheme set the pace and dictated the overall approach to reading.

There seem to be two main factors that changed the ways these teachers worked. One was their growing realisation that there ought to be more to reading than decoding, and that their school reading programmes were essentially based on decoding. The second factor was their feeling that reading at school ought to be more like reading at home, and less of a routine chore.

Bringing about changes in school policy and in practice is slow, and both these teachers realised how important it was to move gradually. Such changes cannot be made overnight, they involve time – time for the staff to agree as a whole on what areas they want to develop, and how developments can be put into effect. School-based INSET meetings were an essential part of the changes in both of these schools, and so were informal contacts with colleagues. The support of the headteacher and of colleagues was vital, particularly in the early stages when both teachers were trying out new approaches in their own classrooms.

For both these teachers long INSET courses, which were held outside the school and which gave them an opportunity to explore ideas in depth and discuss their practice with others, were of the utmost importance. These courses provided them with a knowledge base, introduced them to developments in research and in teaching which they might not otherwise have met, and gave them the confidence to help their colleagues.

Members of staff do look to language coordinators for help and advice, so it is essential for experienced and knowledgeable teachers like these to make their ways of working and their teaching strategies as explicit as possible. In this way their colleagues can understand in detail what they are doing, and why. In these interviews they have described their practice for a wider audience.

For both of these teachers, creating a learning environment where reading is seen as important and enjoyable is a number one priority. The provision and promotion of books is basic to successful teaching and learning. The combination of *providing good books in quantity* and *reading aloud frequently to children* is common to both these classrooms. How books are displayed and organised is an aspect of classroom practice that both teachers attend to, and in their classes children are as familiar as the teacher with the system of organisation.

Both teachers in these discussions mention the importance of helping children to learn to read with *known texts*, and with "*core collections*" of favourite books, where there is more than one copy of the most popular books. Both also mention the key role that *rhyming texts and songs* have played in the developing literacy of the children in their classses. Don Holdaway, in his book *The Foundations of Literacy*, suggested many of these ways of working with young children. His book contains a range of advice, from how often to read aloud to children, to the importance of shared reading in children's literacy activities.

One striking feature of both interviews is the emphasis that both teachers put on a "*three book*" approach in their regular reading aloud sessions. They consciously choose to read *one book the children know well, one that is less familiar, and a new one*, each time. This approach, again, derives from Holdaway and from his plan for familiarising children with books, known as the 'bedtime story' model. For these two teachers, it is an approach which has obviously helped

The teacher's role

children to feel at home with the books available, and has also introduced them to a widening circle of texts.

This 'three book' approach mirrors children's development as readers. This idea is built into the first *Primary Language Record* reading scale. The description of a 'non-fluent reader' on this scale reads as follows:

Tackling known and predictable texts with growing confidence but still needing support with new and unfamiliar ones. Growing ability to predict meanings and developing strategies to check predictions against other cues such as the illustrations and the print itself.

This description makes clear that at any one stage of learning to read a child is at several stages: some aspects of reading are well established and only need to be practised, others are still being learned and consolidated, while others again are new and unfamiliar. By demonstrating to children that reading always involves different levels of experience, and by giving them access to a gradually widening range of texts, these teachers support their independent reading practice, and stress *the value of rereading*.

Both teachers give *systematic support* to children learning to read. Such support includes *regular demonstrations* of reading particular texts, *opportunities to join in with more experienced readers*, opportunities *to discuss texts and to discuss their reading* and advice about what to read next. Their classrooms are organised to give children time and space for reading. In addition, these teachers draw children's attention to the full range of cueing systems and strategies that exist in texts, *encourage them to use all available cues, including grapho-phonic cues,* and help them work out what to do when they meet difficulties.

Both teachers make provision for the bilingual children in their classes and ensure that books in their first languages are available in the classroom. Children are *encouraged to read in their first languages* where they can, and to use their full range of knowledge of language. The teachers are aware that young children may be taking on English as much through their reading as through their talk, and they note the extra importance for developing bilinguals of hearing books read aloud. The collaborative atmosphere in their classroom means that children are used to reading together, and this supports bilingual children's reading in both English and home/community languages.

Parents as partners in their children's learning to read are felt by both teachers to be an essential part of the process, and they speak of *the involvement of parents* in the classroom, as well as in home-school reading schemes, and *Primary Language Record* discussions. They stress the value, too, of *reading records,* and especially of the frameworks provided by the *Primary Language Record*, in enabling teachers to define children's competences as readers more closely, and keep careful track of their progress.

"Real books" are much in evidence in these classrooms and both teachers think that the texts they present children with at the early stages of learning to read are of fundamental importance. Their personal histories show that they have moved to this position because of a profound dissatisfaction with the kinds of reading material that they had to use for teaching reading earlier in their careers. They now want children to understand from the outset that reading is, to quote the Bullock Report, something that other people do for pleasure. They want some of the complex interests and rewards of reading to be present, for children, in its beginnings. Both of them have found that good picture books offer children the most persuasive form of invitation to become a reader.

But neither of these teachers confuses the provision of good children's books with the teaching of reading; they know that books are a medium, and not a method. Their teaching is partly a question of demonstrating constantly to children how reading works and providing them with all the knowledge (of story, written language, and print) that they need to begin to read, and partly a question of helping children to use the knowledge acquired in this way and of monitoring and supporting their independent attempts.

Teachers have many roles to play in the classroom. They are responsible for the provision for reading and for organising the contexts, opportunities and experiences children need to develop as readers. They provide important models for children, and share in their reading as guides, partners, and teachers, ensuring that children are aware of, and are drawing on, all the available sources of information to make sense of texts. They form and sustain partnerships with parents, and thus help children make links between home and school experiences. And as observers and recorders of children's development in reading, in all its aspects, they are in the best position to gather detailed evidence of children's achievements, to make informed qualitative assessments of their progress, and to decide what support and teaching children need next.

A day in the life of a reader

LESLIE
(Year 3; languages: English)

Alison Kelly observed a child in her own class, focussing on the range of reading experiences he has in the course of one day. What is clear from these observations is the important and integral part that writing plays in becoming a reader.

9.15

As usual, day's timetable is on the board. As soon as Leslie comes in he reads the timetable and says

"Why haven't we got P.E. today?" (we usually do, hall is out of use)

Leslie and the rest of the class listen while a child reads aloud the beginning of a story she wrote at home. Another child shares a little book of *My Own Short Old Stories* she also made at home.

9.30-12.00 *Writing workshop*
(with breaks for assembly and play)

Leslie fetches *Tales of Brer Rabbit* (Julius Lester) from book corner and spends some time looking through it, particularly enjoying the illustrations but looking for the different stories as well. "Miss, can I write one of these stories?"

Is very pleased with a new biro he's brought in which he's very keen to write with. Spends the session writing his story *The Lion and the Tiger*.

Reads the title to himself and starts writing straight away. Works persistently, saying words quietly out loud as he writes. Rereads to me once just after he starts (and inserts a full stop for meaning). Later reads to his friend.

Conference with friend:

Jason:
Was he full up?
Did it make him go to sleep?

Leslie:
They always go to sleep after they had their drink.

Jason:
What meat was it?

Leslie:
Lions only eat brown meat.

Jason:
Was he big or small?

Leslie:
The rabbit was the same size as the meat.

Jason:
Did he have a long sleep?

Leslie:
He had a long sleep because it had to take time to do his tummy up.

Jason:
He would have been dead. Did he go and have a sip of water and go off to his friends? You could add that in.

Leslie:
I don't want to add anything because I think it's nice like this.

Jason:
That's like the other one. Did you get the idea from that? Adam's story.

Leslie:
I've got one meself. (referring to *Wolf and Seven Kids*)

Starts to look at spellings

"I know one straight away – night"

12.00 *Sharing time*

Several children share their writing at different stages.

Leslie shares his. Story is enjoyed by children and Adam comments "Taking a big risk!" (with reference to undoing the lion's tummy)

I read *Bringing the Rain to Kapiti Plain* (Verna Aardema, class author of the month), and some poems from *Gargling with Jelly* (Brian Patten).

1.30-2.00 *Quiet reading*

For the first 10 minutes (silent reading time) Leslie reads *Anansi and the alligator eggs* (Evan Jones) to himself.

For the next 20 minutes he shares *Curtis the Hip Hop Cat* (Gini Wade) with a friend. This is a lively and boisterous session where their determination and familiarity with the flow and rhythm of the book sustains their efforts with what is often difficult text.

2.00-3.00 *Week's work*

Goes and fetches an old letter from a pen friend in another school which he reads through. "I wonder what he looks like." Notices the 'r' in 'from' is missing.

Makes a title label for a book he is making connected with the class topic.

Fetches his Week's Work book - checks through to see what he's got to do. Decides on Maths problem.

Fetches card from Maths area - stands and reads it on his own. Brings it over to discuss with me.

Works on problem for rest of session.

3.15-3.45 *Story time*

I read the class a version of *Hip Hop Cat* borrowed from another school. They are delighted by this and instantly want to write their own. We spend 10 minutes arguing about the main character for ours and writing the first verse:

Now this is the story of Karate Cat,

His name is Kitty and he wears a shiny hat,

He's a black belt cat with a real Ninja taste,

He wears his black belt around his waist.

This is surrounded by a lot of lively talk and energetic rereading.

I read a bit from ongoing book **A Strong and Willing Girl** (Dorothy Edwards) which connects with class topic.

The role of the text

'Reading takes pupils beyond first-hand experience: it enables them to project themselves into unfamiliar environments, times and cultures, to gain sympathetic understanding of other ways of life and to experience joy and sadness vicariously. Much of this imaginative experience stems from literature'.

English for ages 5-16

The role of the text

The role of the text in learning to read

This book is based on a premise – the premise that texts matter, that they have a key role to play both in learning to read and in developing as a reader. It also assumes that, in Margaret Meek's phrase, 'texts teach', and that there are 'untaught lessons' about reading that children learn from the books themselves. These are lessons which it might be very difficult to articulate directly, but which form part of the *tacit* knowledge that most experienced readers have about reading. For instance, readers learn that a book is an exercise in suspense; the anticipation that the reader feels when turning from one page to the next in a

picture book is part of the pleasure. Using good children's literature or 'real books' as part of the reading curriculum from the outset, recognises the importance that texts can have in the learning-to-read process.

Yet, in a sense, this is not a new idea. People have never thought that texts *did not* matter in the teaching of reading. In the past, many debates about reading have in fact centred around texts, and the kinds of texts that are likely to support reading development most effectively. The nature of the texts presented to children has, in addition, generally reflected a theory of reading of some kind. In the case of reading schemes, these theories have often been set out in the manuals that have accompanied the schemes, but they have often also been apparent from the very nature of the texts themselves.

Thus, in the eighteenth and nineteenth centuries in England, we find examples of texts based on a theory that learning to read has something to do with learning by rote, which provided easily memorised verses or passages (often from religious books) for this purpose. Many children – and adults – learned to read from the Bible itself, or from the *Church of England Prayer Book*. It was common for children to learn long passages of the scriptures by heart, or to learn the Collect (prayer) for each Sunday by heart.

From these early primers it is also apparent that another theory related to the idea of word-building. Many begin with the alphabet and continue with pages of lists of syllables, often nonsense syllables. There then follow pages of texts composed entirely of monosyllabic words, pages of texts with words of two syllables, and so on.

In the twentieth century we find readers based on phonic principles, with texts designed to practice progressively more difficult blending (an approach that follows directly on from earlier syllabic approaches). Probably the most famous of these were the *Royal Road Readers*. The other main types of reading scheme were those based on look-and-say, the sentence method, or 'keywords' principles, where vocabulary was controlled, continually repeated, and gradually expanded in the belief that learning to read was a straightforwardly incremental process of recognising an ever wider bank of words.

All of these approaches, then, were grounded in theories of reading. The texts constructed for the purpose of practising reading reflected assumptions about what it was that the reader had to do. Two main theories are evident behind these different systems. They are

Page 1	Alphabet, upper and lower case.
Page 2	Alphabet, italic and roman.
Page 3	ba be bi bo bu
	ca ce ci co cu
	da de di do du
	fa fe fi fo fu
Page 5	If ye be I am he
	So we do We to me
	If I go Is it so
	Do I go On we go
Page 9	Tom has got my top
	Can you buy me a new bow
	The man has got a new wig

Extracts from *A Child's Instructor* (1828)

> theories which are based on an atomistic view of the reading process: reading is seen as combining the small constituent parts of text with growing accuracy,

and

> theories which related to memorisation, either of a growing bank of words, or of chunks of text.

The more recent movement towards using children's books as the main medium for teaching reading also reflects a theory. This theory derives from Hallidayan linguistics and a view of semantics as being basic to all language operations – the job that the young reader has to do is to make meaning from text. The implications of this are far-reaching, for reading then becomes not merely a perceptual or mechanical process of word-building, or a simple process of memorisation, but a language and communication process, governed by all the factors that affect all other human communication situations. In Halliday's words

What is learning to read and to write? Fundamentally it is an extension of the functions potential of language. Those children who don't learn to read and write, by and large, are those to whom it doesn't make sense . . . (it) does not match up with their own expectations of what language is for.

The other theoretical reason for foregrounding the importance of good literature in the learning to read process is linked to this, and lies in psycholinguistics, and in all the research that has been done to show how readers do in fact operate with texts. This research shows us readers bringing to texts all their knowledge of language, books, stories, print, and of the world in general, and 'predicting their way through print' making at least as much use of context and meaning (semantic) and language (syntactic) cues as they do of print (grapho-phonic) cues. This process is best supported by texts which offer readers as many normal textual cues as possible, and do not hinder

the brain by leaving out important cues, as the unreal language of some reading schemes does.

Literature-based approaches to the teaching of reading are therefore based on a rejection, and an affirmation. The rejection is of reading scheme material which lacks interest, is hard to find any important meanings in, and which is constructed purely as practice material for decoding. (Bettelheim (1982) quotes two studies that show that many basic reading books had a larger and more demanding vocabulary in the 1920s than they did in the 1960s: "from edition to edition their contents became more boring and repetitious".)

The affirmation is of:

the power that learners have to make sense of meaningful experience and meaningful language (well documented by all work on language acquisition, as well as by psycholinguistic research into reading),

and

the power of good books to engage children's interest and support their attempts to make meaning.

This second point is the topic of this chapter.

Revisiting familiar texts

Superficially, or when it is used in an uncomprehending way, an approach to reading which foregrounds the texts themselves may look like a return to a much earlier style of learning. Bible literacy, as has already been mentioned, was a common form of literacy in the eighteenth and nineteenth centuries in England. The Bible was 'known text'. People knew its characteristic tunes from hearing it read frequently at church and in the family. The stories it held were known stories, and the language was known too. The beginnings of literacy frequently lay in the reading and rereading of texts which were already familiar to the reader. Some groups of children in Britain today still have access to literacy based on sacred texts.

Modern approaches, like Bible literacy, begin with reading aloud, and with texts that are oral 'shared experiences'. But the theory behind this is not a theory of rote learning, although it is true that children do often learn favourite texts by heart. What happens, as learners revisit familiar texts, is that they learn to use all relevant cueing systems from the beginning in their independent attempts to make the texts mean. And as they do so, the less print-dependent cues (e.g. of context, syntax), and their knowledge of the story, support their task of recognising and decoding the print, the part of the reading process in which they are at least experienced. The whole process involves the orchestration of all these different skills; there is a constant interplay between the 'big shapes' in the text and the smaller units which have to be fitted into these shapes. The learner's attention is continually oscillating between the developing meaning and shape of the whole, and the smaller cues in the print; all of these elements are part of the information that readers regularly draw on in approaching a text.

The role of repetition and the place of folk tales

Many people accept psycholinguistic theories of learning to read, and argue that what a reading programme therefore needs are texts that are ones that enable children to use their predictive strategies. (Some modern reading series are founded on this principle). In practice this often means stories with a high proportion of repetition, such as is often found in folktales (e.g. *The Little Red Hen*). But this interpretation is simplistic, and is not an adequate account of what is going on when children learn to read with a favourite story book. Texts that are predictable in their form may be enjoyable or they may be very boring; and whether they are boring or not is likely to depend on other factors than the amount of repetition they involve.

Stories that are truly memorable are often ones that come out of an oral tradition. Folk and fairy tales are stories that have been shaped by centuries of retelling and have therefore had to be memorable. But what makes them memorable is not only the patterning characteristic of oral stories. These familiar tales are powerful in their content too. (see Bettelheim's *The Uses of Enchantment*, 1991), Many of them have archetypal significance, and deal with fantasies and feelings that are part of the inner experience of childhood.

Stories with important themes

Another kind of story that may prove important to children who are learning to read is the kind which deals with strong feelings and significant experiences. Stories like *Angry Arthur* and *Where the Wild Things Are* are of this kind; these explorations of the destructive power of angry feelings, and of the fear of this power, are recognised by many children, as are the feelings of jealousy that are the theme of *John Brown, Rose, and the Midnight Cat*. Similarly, *Not Now, Bernard and Titch* deal with the frustrations and powerlessness of being a child, and being the youngest in a family, while *Peter's Chair, Are You My Mother?*, and *Mr Rabbit and the Lovely Present* focus on the joys and pains of relations with parents and siblings. The writers of such books, it should be pointed out, do not set out to treat strong or problematic feelings directly; like all artists they simply drawn on important emotional material in telling their stories. Books like this can be very important to children, and can help them to understand and come to terms with feelings that might otherwise trouble them. But it is not always easy to predict which books are likely to serve this purpose for which children. Elaine Moss has described how a small book containing an apparently undistinguished story of an adopted kitten became the most important book in her younger daughter's early life, because (as she later realised) it carried a message of supreme significance for this adopted daughter. The texts that children learn to read which are often those that have strong personal meanings for them and that enable them to find themselves in the book, though not of course always in a very obvious or literal way.

Books that reflect a range of languages and cultures

Children read books with their whole selves, and where they cannot do so, where there is nothing in the books available that in any way reflects their worlds, their home lives, their language, or their cultures, they will feel excluded and become discouraged. An important category of books will therefore be those that relate directly to the languages and cultures represented in the school. Despite much discussion of the importance of literature in multicultural education, it remains true that it is not easy to find high quality stories by a range of authors who treat subjects and themes from cultures other than the dominant culture. There are particular difficulties of this kind in relation to stories for very young readers. Booklists such as the *Books for Keeps* guides to *Children's Books in a Multicultural Society* (currently being revised for republication in 1992) can be helpful here, and it will be important to get to know all of the work by writers and author-illustrators

such as John Agard, Molly Bang, James Berry, Madhur Jaffrey, Errol Lloyd and Grace Nicholls, as well as folk stories from the cultures of the classroom, and the full range of books available (e.g. those published by Mantra books, Magi books, National Book Trust, and those available from specialist bookshops). Reviewing journals such as *Dragons' Teeth* can also provide information about what is available, and suggest the criteria by which material can be evaluated.

It should go without saying that in selecting books for the classroom, it will be important to pay attention to the quality of language, illustration and production, as well as to the cultural content and the stories themselves. It will also be important to recognise that stories need not correspond exactly to children's cultural experience in order to reflect it; sometimes children can identify strongly with stories from quite different worlds that correspond emotionally in some way with their own feelings or situations. Where the teacher does not share a language with the children it will also be important to involve other people – support teachers, parents, librarians, booksellers and the children themselves – in making choices for the classroom and ensuring that the books and tapes provided in children's first languages are the best available.

Books that are games

Another category of books that seems important to children beginning to read is made up of those which seem particularly good at teaching the 'game' of reading. Books like *Where's Spot* or *Each, Peach, Pear, Plum* have a special part to play in supporting young readers. These books invite children to join in, either by supplying the next part of the text, exploring the picture, or by finding out what is under the flap – an activity which involves children reading *Where's Spot?* in locating the text to be read. Pop-up books such as *Dear Zoo* and *Dinner Time* have often proved helpful to children without much book experience because they demonstrate the games that books can play particularly well. Some writers or author-illustrators, such as the Ahlbergs, or John Burningham, seem especially aware of what it is that beginning readers need in a text. They show immense aware of what it is that beginning readers need in a text. They show immense ingenuity in demonstrating to children what it involved in reading – for instance, by showing that a story may have two sides (literally) to it, as in *Come Away from the Water, Shirley*.

Books that rhyme

Books like this often feature rhyme, which is very supportive of young readers. Rhyme helps text to be held in the memory, and supports children in their early attempts at independent reading and in the work of matching the words in the head with the words on the page. It is a *highly patterned* form of language, and may help to develop children's linguistic and phonological awareness in that it is language that calls attention to itself. Children may be particularly helped by rhyme and may seek out books in which it features. They can join in the reading of the rhymed text, often by supplying the last, rhyming part of a line (as in *Mr. Magnolia* and *My Cat Likes to Hide in Boxes*) or the refrain (*Don't Forget the Bacon, Brown Bear, Brown Bear*). Bilingual children learning English may be supported by rhyming and memorable texts that teach the rhythms of English. Joining in the reading of such texts represents many children's first way into reading.

Picture books

Picture books are obviously a fundamental category in any reading programme. Jill Bennett's famous booklist, which remains a key resource, was simply called *Learning to Read with Picture Books*. But 'picture books' make too wide a class to generalise about, and it's obviously important to identify, as Jill Bennett does in her publication, those picture books that are specially helpful to young readers, and in which the pictures have an important part to play in the process.

Books that teach the game of reading are built for sharing. Pictures often play a key role in helping understanding, and may even carry an additional story (*Rosie's Walk, Look What I've Got*). This can lead to a division of labour; the child reads the pictures and the adult reads the text. This approach is one that is often spontaneously adopted; it gives both players a part in the game. Children learn to play the games with an adult player, and then by themselves.

Some books for young readers are all pictures. They enable the child to control the whole process of taking meaning from books from the very beginning. Books like *Changes, Changes* or *The Snowman* can be revisited again and again, and during this process children learn essential reading lessons: lessons about the nature of story, the role of narration, anticipation, the twists of a plot, cumulative meanings, and the sense of an ending.

In many modern picture books the text is strongly supported by the pictures, and this can provide a helpful context for children's independent attempts at reading. Pictures can give an extra dimension to the text, adding to the interest of the book and sometimes filling out a minimal text (*How Do I Put It On?*). Or, as in the work of Maurice Sendak, they can create a world around the text that can be explored independently, but which is also an absolutely integral part of the book.

Funny books

Humour is a crucial ingredient in many favourite books; Brian Wildsmith shows how even the simplest of texts can be funny in *The Cat Sat on the Mat*. Funny books enable children to share a joke with the author, which confirms them as members of the 'literacy club'. Jokes like this are capable of being rehearsed and appreciated over and over again; a book like *Dear Zoo* or *That's My Dad* is a source of continual amusement, as well as being an irresistible model for children's own versions. Humorous texts perform an important function for children. Years ago Chukovsky pointed out that young children learn something new about language when they learn how to play with it: that the world can be changed through words alone. Books that show children how these alternative realities can be written down are introducing them to the power of written language, and showing them how the pleasures of imaginative play can be captured and relived. A book that demonstrates this directly is *Maybe it's a Tiger*.

Comic and cartoon books

Children's leisure reading shows that they enjoy illustrated texts and find them helpful; comics allow children to read in a context where text is maximally supported by pictures, and for many children this is a key form of reading practice. Some picture book illustrators use comic techniques – Jan Pienkowski's illustrations for the *Meg and Mog* series, for example, use speech balloons and enormous print for sound effects. These often become an important part of children's early reading repertoire, children greatly enjoy their knockabout humour. The Ahlbergs make good use of cartoon and comic techniques in *Burglar Bill* and *Funnybones*. Techniques like these often permit a text to be read at a variety of levels; adult reads text, children read pictures and balloons. The *Transformers Annual* was a wonderful example of a text that operated on a multitude of levels, with some of the stories in cartoon form, with the option of reading pictures or pictures and text, some that consisted of reading in 'short bursts', and others that were long and elaborate texts full of comic 'high style'. Popular books of this kind often offer interesting lessons about how children can move between different levels of text.

Books that draw attention to written language

Some kinds of books seem specially important in focusing children's awareness of the system of written language and in drawing attention to particular features of language in print. This applies to all levels of written language; alphabet books like John Agard's *Calypso Alphabet* can help to develop awareness of the code, while books like *The Jolly Postman* draw attention to kinds of writing (genres) – the letters and enclosures in the envelopes include many different kinds of text, from fairytale to business letter to mail order catalogue. In addition *The Jolly Postman* shows how an understanding of one story is supported by an understanding of previous story experiences, how texts can refer to each other, and how children can draw on knowledge gained from previous reading. This key lesson in 'intertextuality' is often part of the Ahlberg's work, as for example in *Each Peach Pear Plum*, but it may, unless care is taken to let everyone into the secrets, exclude children whose literary experience is not based on British nursery rhymes and fairy tales.

Another picture book author who seems to have an uncanny gift for teaching children about reading and the written code is Ted Geisler or Dr. Seuss. He accomplishes this by making them laugh a great deal. All his books use rhyme, and introduce a cast of crazy characters (Sam-I-Am, the Cat in the Hat, the Grinch, and inumerable other improbable creatures such as Quilligan Quail, Poozers, Wubbles and Wockets), who get into ludicrous situations. The books go at a breakneck pace, and on the way Dr. Seuss does manage to slip in a few lessons about the ways that sounds are spelled and have cheerful fun with fonics. It's often a relief to children to meet his books, and for some older readers who have had initial difficulties it can be a key experience.

Literary structures

Children often seem to be sensitive to literary structures, and may recall the particularly melodious parts of familiar stories. Literary structures may have the function of acting as 'place-holders' for the words, enabling children to store and recall much bigger chunks of text. Neisser, in *Cognitive Psychology (1967)*, concludes that rhythmic structure is a powerful facilitator of verbal memory. This is what children are drawing on when they play at reading and reenact texts. Subsequently, their well developed knowledge of the text supports them as they begin to refer more closely to the words on the page.

In addition, 'chunking' the text like this enables children to get a sense of the organisation of the whole, and these larger shapes and meanings support their understanding of particular passages. They therefore have at their disposal a wider range of context cues, for they have a much clearer sense of the *whole* context. These are not, of course, skills that children will be able to draw on if the texts they are offered are monotonous in their phrasing and lacking in notable rhythms. One psychologist has expressed concern about the lack of good writing in some materials for young readers. She speculates that children may develop cognitive schemes that correspond to literary structures, and that enable them to organise increasingly complex information:

It seems to me that learning to read must involve the learning of written discourse structures that might, as cognitive organisations, serve to order various aspects of the reading process.

She suggests that predictability and patterned language "may in fact aid the beginner more than the child with more advanced recognition skills". (Bartlett, *1981*)

Literary structures may thus have an essential role to play in supporting the work that the brain has to do as children learn to read, and may be particularly valuable for children who are learning English at the same time as they acquire the written form of the language.

There is now growing evidence that texts which are rhythmical, tuneful, and which contain the kinds of literary structures and patterns that make for memorable language, are better at supporting children's independent attempts at reading. Rhythmic language and rhythmic structures are easier to anticipate than the short, stilted phrases of some reading books, and many children display an enjoyment of literary structures and rhythms. A striking example of a child whose reading progress was closely linked to his pleasure in literary patterns is given in *Inquiry into Meaning* (Bussis et al, *1985*). The authors describe the progress of a six-year-old child who began to read by teaching himself with *Put Me in the Zoo* (a Dr. Seuss book). For the next twelve months he went on reading some Dr. Seuss books but:

No amount of instructional assistance seemed to help him and he could still barely read in November of the second grade. Not until the middle of the year did Josh make a move, and then it was an extremely rapid and dramatic one. His last oral reading sample . . . contains several selections from stories of his own choosing. One of these stories is 'How Perseus and His Mother Came to Seriphos'. It begins as follows:

Once upon a time there were two princes who were twins. Their names were Acrisius and Proetus and they lived in the pleasant vale of Argos, far away in Hellas.

The music of this sophisticated prose can hardly be compared with the verse of 'Put Me in the Zoo', and Josh was such an invisible reader that it is impossible to construct a coherent picture of his progress from one text to the next. The only unifying thread that seems clear is Josh's continuing interest in the sounds and rhythms of language.

The texts to be shared with children need to embody those qualities that seem to be most supportive of learning to read. In addition, of course, a sensitivity to children's choices and to the books that they seem to find particularly worth returning to, will be of great importance. Observing children as they read, independently and together, and keeping careful records of their choices, will enable teachers to document children's individual reading histories, and see the part that texts are playing in their reading progress.

In Part Two of *The Reading Book* we turn theory into practice and look at the implications for classrooms of the perspectives on reading outlined in Part One. The practices and approaches described in Part Two include all the elements that would need to appear in a school's reading policy.

Teaching approaches: i

The teaching approaches described in this section are divided into two main types:

i) approaches that develop children's awareness of the 'big shapes' in texts (overall meaning, written language structures, story), and

ii) approaches that draw attention to the smaller units in text, to words and to letter-sound relationships.

All of the approaches outlined in the first part of the section have one thing in common. They demonstrate what reading is about and they enable children to join in the whole activity from early on. They stress meaning, enjoyment, and familiarity with the tunes, patterns and rhythms of written language and of particular texts. They are also all 'context-support' approaches (Morris, 1963) in which the reader is given maximum support in reading a text, support which can gradually be reduced or withdrawn as the child becomes a more confident and independent reader.

Reading aloud

'...... reading aloud to children is of the utmost importance in supporting their development as readers.'

Primary Language Record Handbook.

There is strong evidence to show that being read to is a key experience in children's learning to read. Gordon Wells' Bristol Language Development Project found that listening to stories was significantly associated with children's development both as readers and as writers.

Reading aloud to children can be a whole-group or group activity, or a one-to-one experience. In the early stages of learning to read children may need to be read to very frequently, at least two or three times a day. Children who are read to regularly are acquiring a lot of the knowledge they need to help them become independent readers: knowledge of the tunes and patterns of written language, knowledge of the language of books, knowledge of story structures, and familiarity with a growing range of texts. When they choose these books to read independently, they already have

A core of books

'We were taken once a week to the local library and I recall being tremendously overwhelmed by the number of books there and I really didn't know what to choose or how to choose.'

(A teacher's reading history)

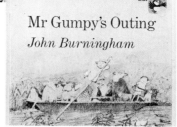

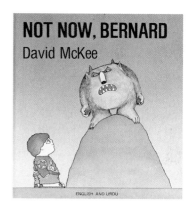

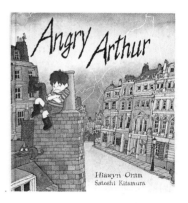

Choice can be confusing. Some teachers feel that in classrooms where there is no set reading scheme, more thought needs to be given to what books children are introduced to, and what books are emphasised in the reading programme. One solution is to select a 'core of books', which then become part of the repertoire of the class. Teachers can support children's reading of these books in a variety of ways:

- by making them the basis of the 'reading aloud' programme, and rereading them frequently

- by providing multiple copies of these key books

- by buying or making 'big books' of the texts

- by providing taped versions of the books in the listening corner

- by exploring the stories of the books through dramatic or artistic activities (the classroom could contain a model boat, for Max to sail away in, or a table-top model of Rosie's farmyard, for her to take her walk around)

- by hearing children read these well-known texts and talking regular reading samples of their progress. This offers a structured way of charting children's development as readers.

Choosing the books that will make up this core of texts could be a valuable activity for an infant staff group. Such an activity makes you think about which books seems to have been specially important in children's learning to read, and what it is about those books that makes them particularly powerful. Any selection eventually arrived at is likely to include traditional stories *(The Three Billy Goats Gruff, Who's in Rabbit's House)*, classic picture-story books *(Rosie's Walk, Where the Wild Things Are)*, books which incorporate rhyme *(Each Peach Pear Plum, Ten Nine Eight)*, books that reflect children's linguistic and cultural backgrounds *(Calypso Alphabet, The Old Woman and the Rice Thief)*, humorous books *(Not Now Bernard, The Fat Cat)*, and books that enable children to join in the reading *(Where's Spot?, Brown Bear Brown Bear)*. A selection of about thirty books should provide an adequate core of books for an infant classroom, but there will need to be more than one copy of these frequently revisited texts.

Though any such list of texts will need to be continually revised, and though these will never be the only books shared in the classroom, it may help both teachers and children to have a common core of books that all the class are familiar with, and that support the learning and the teaching of reading.

---

a good knowledge of the context, and this supports their early independent attempts.

In Liz Waterland's *Read with me* she describes this as 'an apprenticeship approach to reading'. Children who are read to on a one-to-one basis in this way soon begin to join in the reading, perhaps echoing the teacher's reading, and to supply words or phrases that they know or recognise. Gradually they become confident to take over more of the reading of these well-known texts for themselves.

Reading aloud to children goes on being important even when they can read confidently for themselves, and needs to continue throughout a child's primary schooling. This is the main way that teachers can introduce new books, and new kinds of books, to the class, and will be a major factor in their reading development. Information books as well as fiction books need to feature in reading-aloud sessions – children need support with the less familiar style of information prose.

Keeping a record of books that have been read in this way, to the class and to individuals, and rereading favourite books often, will ensure that the reading aloud programme has coherence and continuity, and that children have opportunities to revisit these texts. Time for reading aloud is precious, and teachers will need to plan how to spend it; they may want to consider approaches like those described in *A core of books*, or *Holdaway's 'bedtime story' model*.

A permanent listening corner, with storytapes and accompanying books (commercially produced or home-made) enables children to hear those favourite books again or meet new books, and practise their reading independently.

Holdaway's 'bedtime story' model

In Don Holdaway's book *The Foundations of Literacy*, the author considers how books that parents have shared with children, as bedtime stories or favourite books, can become the basis of their own playing at reading, their reenactments of texts, and eventually of their learning to read independently. Holdaway stresses that the regular sharing of certain books is only half the picture; the other half is children's independent practice with familiar texts, and their reenactments of known stories. His book applies this 'developmental model' to the classroom. He suggests ways of introducing books – often through shared reading sessions – which children can join in the reading of, and subsequently re-read independently, in the way described in *A Core of Books*.

Holdaway considers how this approach can be implemented in a methodical way in the infant classroom. He describes the stages by which children move from *discovery* of a new text, in which they get to know the story and begin to participate in the reading, to *exploration* of the text, through rereadings and through activities related to the book, to *independent experience and expression,* when children are encouraged to read or reenact the text independently or with friends. Throughout these stages Holdaway stresses the

Using songs and rhymes

'Each Peach Pear Plum
I spy Tom Thumb'

One of the things that many successful children's books have in common is rhyme. Often such rhyming books have a particular importance for children's learning to read. Books such as the Rosemary Wells' *Noisy Nora*, Quentin Blake's *Mr. Magnolia* and Bill Martin's *Brown Bear Brown Bear* are all rhyming texts, while one of the most successful reading teachers of all time, Dr. Seuss, works almost exclusively in rhyme.

It is easy to see why rhyme is helpful to young readers. Rhyme makes text memorable, and enables children to join in the reading experience more readily. Highly patterned text provides extra cues for children who are learning to read; rhyming or rhythmical texts help children who are beginning to be able to read the print, but who are also using a mixture of memory and prediction in their independent reading.

Songs offer even more supportive cues through their tunes, and many children in the past must have learnt reading from singing hymns. There are so many good children's songs that can be sung together, following the words on a flip chart, or which can be made into Big Books, or recorded on cassette and stored in the listening corner, with copies of the words in a song book, or on a set of song cards. This effective and pleasurable way of supporting children's reading is currently underused in schools, yet it provides maximal context support to beginning readers and is also greatly enjoyed by children.

way in which children's attention can be drawn to letter-sound relationships and the structure of words, in the context of the reading.

Holdaway's approach has much in common with Liz Waterland's *apprenticeship approach to reading*, though he places less emphasis on the teacher reading one-to-one with the child, and more or shared reading experiences with groups and with the whole class. *Shared Reading* is the best known translation into practice of Holdaway's method.

Other teachers have considered how best to structure their book-based reading programmes. The 'three-book approach' in which, at each reading-aloud session, several times a day, the teacher reads *one new book, one book that has been heard before,* and *one old favourite,* is another way of ensuring that children have opportunities to revisit key texts frequently, but are also continually being introduced to new reading experiences.

DON HOLDAWAY

THE FOUNDATIONS OF LITERACY

Language experience approaches

Language-experience approaches to reading go back a long way, but were formalised in the USA in the early sixties. The essential features of the approach were:

- children's speech, reading and writing were linked in an integrated approach to reading
- children's accounts of personal experiences were dictated to the teacher
- these written texts then became the main source of reading material for the child.

Children's texts were often dictated in group sessions and recorded on a flip chart or a 'language-experience' chart. In Britain, the method of using a child's own words as the basis of a reading programme was formalised in *Breakthrough to Literacy*. *Breakthrough* was not always popular with teachers because the materials were sometimes complicated to organise. Though it could support children's reading development, it sometimes constrained their writing; composition could be limited to one sentence, and children's language was often restricted by the words available in their Sentence Makers.

However, the principle of learning to read through writing, through dictating texts to the teacher, or composing independently, is an important one; such approaches mean that children are always working with meaningful known text, and they lead children to look carefully at grapho-phonic relationships.

Modern developments from language-experience approaches include the publishing of children's own stories, which then become part of the reading stock of the classroom. Book-making is now, in many schools, a major influence on children's reading progress. In some classrooms, children's published stories are also recorded on cassette, and included in the listening corner. Language-experience approaches now take their place alongside other ways in to reading in modern classrooms, and are often found to be particularly helpful to children who are experiencing difficulties in getting started with their reading.

Shared Reading

'What a child can do with assistance today, she will be able to do by herself tomorrow' (Vygotsky, *Mind in Society*).

Don Holdaway is credited with introducing the practice of shared reading in a systematic way into the infant classroom. He began to use enlarged texts – Big Books – regularly, so as to enable children to see the print as they took part in reading-aloud sessions. Later, children were encouraged to reread these texts with a friend, or in a small group.

Holdaway used shared reading to reproduce in the classroom the conditions for successful home learning. He emphasised the importance of corporate and collaborative experiences in learning. Rehana Alam, in a recent CLPE publication *Shared Reading, Shared Writing,* stresses the value of shared reading for children who are not confident readers: 'I found that those children who always hesitated to read, read the text confidently because they were sharing the book with the others'. Bilingual children who are new to English may be particularly helped by this supported activity.

Shared reading is also a good context in which to begin to focus analytically on print and notice grapho-phonic cues. Teachers can encourage children to look for particular features in the text, such as letters from their names, or to find words that begin similarly. Often children initiate this, as they begin to notice letters and words that they recognise, and work out relationships.

All that is needed for shared reading is a collection of enlarged texts – home-made versions of well-known stories, stories written by the class, or commercially produced Big Books. Any teacher who is using a core of books as part of her reading programme will probably want to ensure that most of them are available in the classroom in a large format. A list of Big Books is provided in *Shared Reading, Shared Writing* (CLPE), which also contains other articles on this approach to literacy.

Teaching approaches: ii

The second part of this section reviews on the most effective ways of helping children to focus on print, on letter-sound relationships, and on how words are written. It suggests both direct and indirect ways in which children's growing knowledge of print cues can be supported. The links with their developing writing will be particularly important to this aspect of their reading.

Names

One of the commonest ways for children to become aware of print and of letter-sound relationships is through a growing awareness of names: their own at first, and then other people's. Names are around in all classrooms, on children's trays, on their books, on the displays of their work, and teachers' registers and records. As children listen to stories from books, teachers point out the authors' and illustrators' names, and sometimes these names are the same as those of children in the classes. Names become a way into print, a constant reminder of the links between letters and sounds, and an important site for learning more about these relationships. Ferreiro and Teberosky refer to children's names as the 'first stable string' of letters that they become aware of. Anne Washtell has described how frequently her class of reception infants referred to names in the early stages of reading and writing. Names constituted important information bank for them in their developing awareness of print:

Corah read to herself for twenty minutes looking at several books. She kept returning to Story Chest's I Want an Ice Cream*, paying close attention to the word "ice". Finally she commented "Ice is in Alice."*(Washtell 1989)

Teachers can encourage children to use their knowledge of names, to play games with the names of the children in the class, grouping them according to their initial sounds or making them the basis of an alphabet. Bilingual children whose names are written in a different script in their first language can demonstrate the two ways of writing their name; discussion of what they know about different language systems will enable them to make links between them, and enhance language awareness within the class.

is the Punjabi alphabet

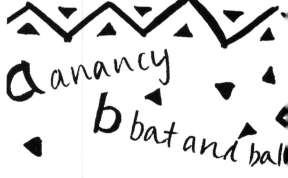

Making alphabets

Alphabets are a basic resource in an infant classroom - both commercially produced alphabet books, of which there are now some dazzling examples, and books produced in the classrooms and by individuals. Alphabets in other forms, such as plastic and magnetic letters, also need to be provided and used. A growing knowledge of the alphabet brings with it an increasing awareness of the relationship between the name of the letters and their sounds. The use of the word processor is often a very effective way of fostering this awareness. It is helpful to know letter names from an early stage, because this provides children with a means of talking about what they are beginning to discover about written language.

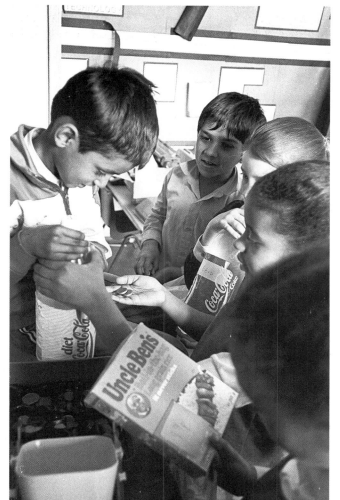

Print in context

Many children can read print in context, even if they cannot always read it when it occurs in isolation. Harste, Burke and Woodward found that ten out of twelve six year olds could read the word CREST when they were shown it on a toothpaste tube (the other two read TOOTH-PASTE). Teachers can provide children with abundant examples of these kinds of 'texts in contexts' in the classrooms, and encourage them to draw on the knowledge of print they acquire in reading familiar signs and slogans. Any infant classroom can make print important and interesting by featuring labels, announcements, favourite titles, and texts that teacher and children have created together. Short memorable texts like rhymes, jingles, proverbs, riddles, and favourite jokes, will provide entertaining ways for children to gain more knowledge of written language and of relations between letters and sounds.

Letters and sounds

Demonstrating the links between letters and sounds is often done in real contexts, but teachers can also draw attention to these relationships directly. In shared reading, children can be encouraged to look for particular letters or letter combinations and find words beginning with these letters. Cloze-type games, in which words are masked to encourage guessing from context, and from initial letter cues, can be played.

In shared writing, children can tell the teacher how they think words begin and end, and work out spellings using ideas about how sounds are spelled, and how words look. They can also occasionally make lists of words that begin similarly and compose texts based on alliteration.

Displays, collections and home-made posters can highlight particular letters and sounds that have been discussed in the classroom. Initial consonants will be most easily taken on, and there will need to be discussion about the different ways that vowels are used and about more complex combinations of letters, with children finding examples. Children can be invited to add to displays, to compile their own, or to make scrapbooks and picture books featuring the letter-sound combinations that they know. The important thing will be to create an awareness of how words are made, so that children begin to attend more consciously to the features of words. This information will be much more actively drawn on in their own independent writing.

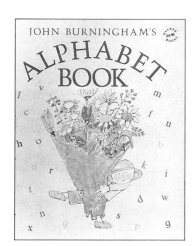

Alphabet books made in the classroom can be more responsive to the cultures and languages of the children in the class, and can include alphabets, syllabaries and sets of ideograms from scripts other than English. Apart from alphabets of children's names, there can be alphabets about food, dress and other culturally influenced aspects of life. Alphabets can draw on what the children in the classroom collectively know about written language. One Coventry teacher compiled a 'Delicious Alphabet' for children in her class, made up of real food labels for food suggested by the children. The word processor program known as 'The Animated Alphabet' is another useful resource.

1

Rhymes and jingles

Just as rhyming texts can support young readers' early attempts at reading, so rhymes can serve a particularly important function by directing their attention to the shapes and sounds of words, and how those sounds are written down. Bradley and Bryant(1985) found that a knowledge of nursery rhymes was a good predictor of the ease with which children learned to read, and suggested that, through rhymes like these, children were developing phonological awareness and a sensitivity to the sounds and features of words. They draw on this awareness when they begin to associate sounds and letters, and match the way words sound with the way they look and are spelled. All kinds of rhymes and songs, as well as nursery rhymes, including rhymes and songs in languages other than English, can support this kind of growing awareness of phonology. Poetry and rhyme have a high degree of pattern and the beginnings and endings of words are important in this kind of patterning; initial letters may be alliterated, and word endings chime or rhyme. Through texts like these, children's attention can be drawn to the beginnings and endings of words and to the games that language can play. Rhymes can become part of the repertoire of the class, and be made into posters and big books for sharing. In this way children can begin to practise their growing grapho-phonic knowledge in easy and pleasurable ways.

Rhyming language is language that draws attention to itself. Dr. Seuss's work plays games with rhymes, and these games make opaque features of language that are normally transparent and hard to see. In addition Seuss exploits the meaninglessness that results from focusing on the sounds of words alone; several of his books work by playing with phonically regular language, and using it to create deliberate nonsense. This is a great deal better than distorting a story by attempting to write it in phonically regular language, as the writers of some reading schemes try to do.

And some very fat owls
who are learning to hoot —
But Mr Magnolia
has only one boot.

from *Mr Magnolia* by Quentin Blake
Cape/ Picture Lions

Writing and Shared Writing

It's above all through writing that children become conscious of the relationship between the sounds of words and the way they are written down. Teachers who regularly use shared writing as a way of supporting children's literacy development notice that children are often intensely interested in seeing how words they know are encoded. In shared writing session children will often spontaneously remark on the features of written language, including such things as upper and lower case, and punctuation marks, and will point out letters from their name, other letters they know, or offer spellings. Teachers are able to draw parallels with words children already know, and draw attention to the ways words are constructed and spelled. Activities like these offer a strong basis for the development of grapho-phonic knowledge.

When children compose together, working on large sheets of paper or at the word processor,

Word games and wordplay

Word games draw attention to language and to sounds of words and the way they are constructed. Some games focus usefully on particular features of language, eg composing alliterative texts or stories. Here is a selection of games that many teachers say they would not be without in their classrooms, or which they play regularly with children both for fun and as a way of developing their grapho-phonic knowledge:

● *I Spy* offers endless practice in identifying initial letter sounds.

● *Hangman* develops children's awareness of word making, and provides a strong motivation for accurate spelling. It can be played with single words or in more elaborate ways with phrases and sentences. At this point it becomes more like . . .

● *Devtray*, an excellent computer program for encouraging children to use the same mixture of contextual cues combined with grapho-phonic knowledge. Children's own texts can be included in the texts to be 'developed'.

● *Boggle* is a game, which like many informal games with words, involves children in thinking of the different words than can be made up from the letters available.

● *Scrabble* is a family favourite that can usefully be adopted in the classroom. Players need to be aware of how letters can be combined and recombined, and the game increases their awareness of vocabulary.

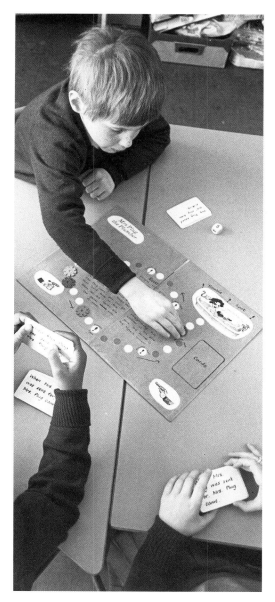

they are similarly engaged in pooling their knowledge of the writing system and of what words look like and how they are spelled.

As children begin to write for themselves, when they are inventing or 'having a go' at spellings from an early stage, they are constantly faced with the question of how words are written down. It has been found that children who are used to writing independently demonstrate greater phonological awareness than children who are used to copying under teachers' writing. It will sometimes be helpful to discuss children's independent spellings with them, to compare them with adult spellings, and to talk about letter-sound relationships and the different ways that words and sounds can be spelled. If some time is given to the study of spelling patterns and children are encouraged to attend to the shapes and features of words, their growing knowledge of how words are constructed will support their reading.

Word collections

In addition to games, there exist all kinds of ways of focusing on the shades of meaning in words, and the way words are constructed. It's often helpful to make a collection of words in connection with a particular topic, or as a word bank to support children's writing. Word collections can also be used as a means of word study, with words being drawn together in families, or on the basis of their patterning. Children's reading can be supported by an awareness of the way words are built up and of the function of common prefixes and suffixes.

Teachers can make word collections with children in shared writing sessions, or groups of children can make their own collections and present them on posters. Posters and displays of this kind then become part of the resources of the classroom. Activities like this can lead, with older children, to the wider study of words and their etymologies and meanings, the use of thesauruses, and so on.

Hearing children read

The teaching approaches described in this section draw children's attention to the different kinds of information contained in text - both the high level information (semantic and syntactic cues, literary styles and rhythms), and the low-level information (grapho-phonic cues, spelling). As they learn to read, children will begin to draw on all these different kinds of information. Teachers hearing children read can observe the strategies they are using and direct their attention to other cues if necessary. Record-keeping (e.g. a running record or informal assessment as part of a Primary Language Record reading sample) will help to focus observations.

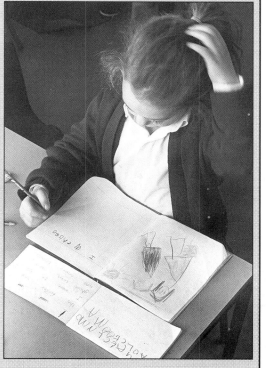

2 Book making and publishing

Writing and publishing children's books in the classroom bring together a number of important aspects of children's literacy development. Children can draw on their experiences of play, story, drawing and spoken language in ways that directly reflect their own interests, languages and cultures. Written language becomes meaningful through children's construction of their own texts. Bookmaking helps children to develop as authors; this experience of writing will be drawn on in their reading. In this way, book making supports children at all stages of reading and writing, but is particularly helpful to bilingual children who are learning English and to children who have reading, writing and learning difficulties.

Access to good models

If children are to become successful and confident authors they need access to a wide variety models for their writing. Teachers need to provide:

● **access to a wide range of books** in the class and school library including picture books, pop-up and flap books, books in different languages and scripts, poetry, rhymes, folk tales from many cultures, information books, autobiographies, contemporary stories, science fiction books, texts written by authors from a range of cultures, children's novels

● **opportunities for shared and paired reading,** group reading of big books and books with multiple copies

● **frequent opportunities for oral story telling** – telling stories, listening to stories told by other children, parents, teachers and librarians, and visiting storytellers.

A reading aloud policy enables children to get to know a wide range of books and stories.

A wide range of models can be used as starting points for children's book writing. Folk tales in a variety of traditional forms provide excellent starting points. Some good examples include:
Seasons of Splendour, Tales, Myths and Legends of India (Madhur Jaffrey)
The bird who was an elephant (Aleph Kamal)
Journey with the Gods (Linda Shanson and Anita Chowdry), in English and Bengali versions (including tape)
The Hobyahs (Simon Stern, from the original by Joseph Jacobs)
The White Crane (Junko Marimoto)

Closely patterned folk tales like *A Story, A Story* (pattern of three), *Who's in Rabbit's house?* (a traditionally repetitive story building up to a surprise ending) and *Why mosquitoes buzz in peoples' ears* (a cumulative story), all by Verna Aardema, provide excellent and memorable models for children's books.

Support for the book making process

Modelling the process
Teachers should make explicit the process that goes into making a book (eg. thinking and talking about ideas, planning, drafting and redrafting planning illustrations and layout. The classroom should be organised in a way which makes it possible for children to work in this way and there should be clear routines for everyone to follow. It is important that children feel they have sustained time to explore ideas, revise work, and to write out, illustrate and design their books.

Shared writing
Grouping children around a flip chart with a teacher provides valuable opportunities for children to join in the writing in a supported context and allows for informal talk about the construction of stories and texts, and about features such as vocabulary, punctuation, layout, plots and characters.

Collaborative work
Book making offers wonderful opportunities for

Some books help to show how a particular genre works. Among these are *The Dark Dark Tale* (various versions), which shows the techniques of building up suspense; *Three up a tree* (James Marshall), where three children tell each other taller and taller stories; and *The True Story of the Three Little Pigs by A Wolf* (Jon Scieszka), where a new story is created from a familiar one by taking the standpoint of a different character.

Certain well-loved books such as *Not Now Bernard* (David McKee) or *The Hungry Caterpillar* (Eric Carle) can be used directly as models for re-tellings, or can be transposed into a different setting with different characters. Others, like *The Jolly Postman* (Janet and Allan Ahlberg), provide an opportunity to explore the intertextuality of stories – in this case in the form of letters of different kinds: invitations, adverts, business letter, postcards, and so on.

Rhyming books of all kinds, such as *Each Peach Pear Plum* (Janet and Allan Ahlberg) or *Bringing the Rain to Kapiti Plain* (Verna Aardema) are often favourites. Children might undertake their own rhyming stories, perhaps in shared writing so that they do not spend too long searching for a rhyme. There is an enormous range of poetry to inspire children to write their own poems, including titles such as *Come into my tropical garden* (Grace Nicholls), *Mother gave a shout* (Morag Styles and Susanna Steele, *Where the sidewalk ends* (Shel Silverstein), *When I Dance* (James Berry), and *Speaking for ourselves* (Hiawyn Oram).

Graphic novels based on children's experiences of cartoon books and comics are a new and popular genre, and show children how to manage quite sophisticated narratives using texts and pictures. Similarly, information books like *The Way Things Work* (David Macaulay) or *Scripts of the world* (Suzanne Bukiet) show different ways in which information can be presented.

children to work together in a wide range of groupings and settings : with a partner, in a small or larger group, or in a whole class setting. Children can work with regular writing partners; they can be grouped with others of similar or different abilities, according to gender, in mixed language groups, or with others who speak the same first language. The important lessons here come from watching and working with others, and from being both a writer and an audience, as writing is tried out on peers during the process of writing and not only at the end of it.

Developing strategies for independent writing
It is important that children have strategies of this kind so that they can work as independently as possible. This makes time for teachers to give children more sustained individual attention. It is useful, for example, for the whole class to decide together on ways of finding out how to spell words, ways which don't involve asking adults in the room. E.g:

- write the first letter and any others you can think of
- write what you think and come back to it later
- ask a friend
- use a dictionary (a variety, at different levels of complexity, should be available)
- look for words around the room
- use a 'have-a-go' word book

Supporting bilingual children
Book making provides a wide variety of ways to support languages other than English in the classroom. 'In house 'publications are much more flexible than bought materials and can be tailored precisely to meet the needs of children in the class. The help of bilingual support teachers, parents, and other biliterate children in the school will be valuable here. It is important that single and dual language texts be produced in ways that do not subordinate all other languages to the patterns and conventions of English.

A sense of audience

As writing and publishing books becomes part of the ethos of the classroom and the school, children's sense of audience can develop by writing for children in their own class, with regular readings not only of new books, but of work in process, in writers' workshops. They can also tape books and stories for others in the class and school to listen to. It can be valuable for children to share books with other classes – for example children who are having difficulties can gain status and self-esteem from reading their books aloud to younger children.

Children's own books can be integrated into class and school libraries and displayed alongside commercially published books. Children can then take these books home to read to parents. Books can be advertised through posters and displays and by being read in assemblies. Books can also be displayed in local community centres and libraries, either on their own or as part of other exhibitions. This kind of access to a wider readership will help children to become aware of the needs of different audiences.

2

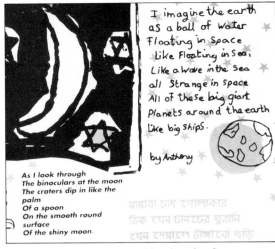

I imagine the earth
as a ball of water
Floating in Space
Like Floating in Sea,
Like a wave in the Sea
all Strange in space
All of these big giant
Planets around the earth
Like big ships.

by Anthony

As I look through
The binoculars at the moon
The craters dip in like the palm
Of a spoon
On the smooth round surface
Of the shiny moon.

যামারা চাঁদ গোলাকার
ঠিক যেন চামচের ঘ্রাণি
যেন দেয়ালে টাঙানো ঘড়ি

Happenings in Poem Talk!, by class 6 at Grasmere Primary School, Hackney with help from Simon Spain, Susanna Steele and Penny Robertson, 1991

A variety of forms

As well as story, children's books can take a variety of forms across a wide range of learning contexts:

- a class anthology of prose or poems, which may be focused on a class topic
- joke books
- books based on cartoons or comics
- personal histories or accounts – these could include parents' histories and stories
- information books in a variety of forms involving non-narrative writing
- accounts of activities across the curriculum, e.g. books that summarise conclusions, diaries that monitor change over time in science activities
- books based on photographs
- taped books – including books written in more than one language. Children may take different parts on the tape, one playing narrator, others taking the parts of characters. Children's own books and tapes can be stored alongside the 'published' book and tape collection in the classroom.

Every family has some camels, because when we have to move we put everything from the house on the camels. My mother's family has 20 camels.

Somali homes a spiral bound information book in English by Roda Ahmed from Harrington Hill Primary School in Hackney

The Cockerel & the Hen

The Cockerel & the Hen

મરઘો અને મરઘી

The cockerel and the Hen, by Sunil Patel and edited by Robert Hewitt 10yrs., Harlesden Primary School, Brent Young Writers Series

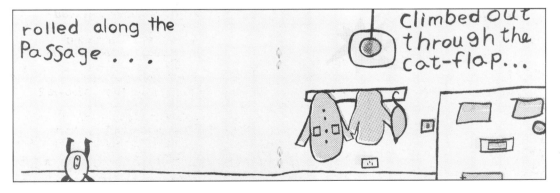

rolled along the Passage . . .

Climbed out through the cat-flap . . .

Baby Tony, by Tony Morgan 9yrs. Brentfield JM&I School, *Brent Young Writers* Series

went Past the dustbin and ginger cat . . .

out through the blue gate . . . .

Design

There are a wide variety of ways of making books. (*A Book of One's Own* (Paul Johnson) and *Making Books Made Easy* (Olwyn Burgess) give helpful suggestions about this.) Some of the main formats are:

- zig-zag books
- books with slide-on binders
- spiral bound books
- stapled spine books in a variety of shapes and sizes
- books cut out in different shapes to reflect the story
- sewn books - both large and elaborate and smaller, less formal ones
- pop-up and lift-the-flap books which can be used to stimulate writing through play
- multi-sensory books which can include feeling and smelling experiences as part of the text (The Library for the Handicapped Child has some good examples.)

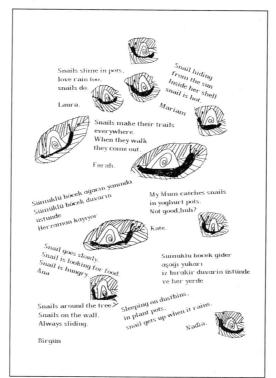

What's Going On? Poems by class 5 Grasmere Primary School, Hackney, with help from Susanna Steele, Penny Robertson and Tozün Issa, 1989.

'I was seven when I wrote this book. I'm eight now. I like drawing pictures and making stories. This book took me a few days. First I read a few books, then I thought about my story.
I did some writing, then more writing. Then a drawing, then more writing and another drawing. I wasn't sure what was going to happen in the end. I thought about it as I went along'
If I had a magic washing machine, by Sanjay, a simple published zig-zag book from the Brent Young Writers Series

Levels of publication

A number of levels of publication can be explored, from a one-off big production – which may be a hardback, elaborately covered and presented book to which many children have contributed – to individual books. These can take a variety of forms, and can be very simply produced, or quite elaborate. Multiple copies can be made by photocopying, and these can be taken home while the original stays in the class library or remains in the care of the author.

Teachers can sometimes gain access to printing, laminating and book-binding facilities to enhance book production. Short biographies of the authors, with photographs, can be included on the back covers of books. Printing need not be difficult to organise with the desk-top publishing programs now available, and good-quality photocopying can provide excellent results when books are being produced in smaller numbers. Books can be photocopied or printed and published either on a limited basis or in larger quantities (with ISBN numbers allocated) as part of a class, school or borough project (see **Brent Young Writers Series, Hackney Publishing Project**).

Useful information
- *A Book of One's Own* *Developing literacy through making books* Paul Johnson
- *Making Books Made Easy* a short, pamphlet by Olwyn Burgess, available from CLPE.
- *Shared Reading, Shared Writing* CLPE
- 'Story and Storytelling' *Language Matters* Issue 2/3 1988
- 'Information Books' *Language Matters* Issue No 2 1990
- **Caxton Programme and Handbook** available from ILECC John Ruskin Street London SE5 OPQ

Books for children about books and publishing
- *The story of a picture book* Rodney Martin and John Siow
- *Make Your Own Pop-ups* Joan Irvine – mainly about making cards but works with books as well.
- *Making a book* Ruth Thomson, which features the work of Anthony Browne
- *How a book is made* Aliki
- *Books* Tim Merrison
- *How a BOOK is made* A Puffin Resource Pack Penguin Books Ltd, Harmondsworth Middlesex

3 Providing books; promoting reading

These pages confront the practical issues that face schools when they review their bookstock and reorganise their libraries or book corners. Questions of choosing, buying and displaying books are linked to ideas about how reading can be promoted most effectively within the school, so that children can gain maximum access to books.

Allocating money for books

Priorities for spending need to be discussed by the staff as a whole. An informal survey, undertaken periodically, of all existing stocks in school library and classroom collections may expose neglected areas, for which special provision can be made.

The school library is best seen as a pool from which classroom teachers can draw when their own collections are inadequate for particular purposes – topic work for instance. It can also house expensive reference books of which a school has only one copy.

The classroom library will probably include a small core collection – which may need revision from time to time – of best known, best loved, titles which teachers rely on and children return to again and again. In addition to these, a wider range of books, both fiction and non-fiction, will be needed to support curriculum work and to enable children to read more widely.

Money allocated to books ought to be seen as provision for learning across the curriculum rather than just 'reading' or 'library' expenditure. Picture books like Pamela Allen's *Who Sank the Boat* and *Mr. Archimedes' Bath* are the science books of the younger children.

Finding out about books

Schools often need help in finding out what books are available and where to obtain them. LEA school library services (where they exist) can help both with selection and ordering. They can also provide short term loan collections. Sometimes, when loan services are not available, the local public library can help.

The staff can help each other increase the bank of books they know by presenting books they have used successfully to their colleagues in staff meetings. INSET with language postholders or advisory staff is another source of information and advice – better than relying on publishers' representatives with their obvious bias in favour of their own materials.

The whole staff could make occasional visits to teachers' centres and exhibitions, museum collections, the school library service displays and local bookshops. For those schools within visiting distance, an outing to the Centre for Language in Primary Education enables teachers to browse in a library of over 25,000 books, and to see new titles as well as books published less recently. If the school subscribes to the CLPE journal *Language Matters*, visits are free of charge.

Also in London, the children's collection at Book Trust contains all children's books published with-

Provision

To ensure a 'good standard of provision' schools should spend between £19 and £20 per pupil per year on books. Between £16 and £17 would give a 'reasonable standard.' *

Provision should be made for around 10% of the total stock to be replaced annually, for lost, damaged, worn out or out of date books. H.M. Inspectorate suggest a minimum workable level of 8 books per pupil, with 10 per pupil being regarded as adequate.

See *The Book Check Action File* (available from Book Trust, £1.95) for a helpful guide to assessing a school's book needs.

* Recommendations drawn up by Book Trust and the Educational Publishers Council for 1989-1990, with an allowance made for inflation. A more recent decision suggests that under LMS, 2% of the total budget would be a reasonable aim for expenditure on books.

Questions to ask about classroom collections

What kind of range is there?
Are all the children's needs being met?
Are different genres represented, e.g. family stories, adventure stories, ?
Are all the school's home/community languages represented?
Does the core collection need revision?
Are there enough books to satisfy the more experienced readers?
Are there books which will appeal to both boys and girls?
If children are taking books home, are there enough books to choose from?
Are Big Books used and are there enough small copies for the children?
Are there taped stories? With the printed versions?
Are there stories in different formats (e.g. video, tape/slide)?
Are children's own books (perhaps printed and laminated where possible) included in the collection?
Is supporting material available (e.g. puppets, other artifacts)?
Do the books provided support National Curriculum requirements as outlined in the Programmes of Study?

in the past two years. Schools may also like to know that the Poetry Library on the fifth floor of the Festival Hall can be visited freely. Formalities are minimal, children are welcome and books may be borrowed.

Printed book lists can be bought and kept in the staff room; the Thimble Press Signal guides for example, and Letterbox Library's monthly lists and their back lists. (The Thimble Press publication *The Reading Environment, How Adults Help Children Enjoy Books* by Aidan Chambers discusses all the issues raised in this section comprehensively and thoughtfully.) The periodical *Books For Keeps* should be in every school, as should *Dragons Teeth* and the *School Librarian*. This last comes as a result of membership of the School Library Association, a useful organisation for a school to subscribe to for its help in managing and developing school libraries. (eg. *School Libraries: Steps in the Right Direction*. Guidelines for a school library resource centre; (1989).

Teachers may need help selecting titles for the dual language and community language book collection. Sometimes community language teachers or parents can be involved, sometimes community helpers are willing to give advice.

Reading should include picture books, nursery rhymes, poems, folk tales, myths, legends and other literature which takes account of pupil's linguistic competences and backgrounds. Both boys and girls should experience a wide range of childrens literature. Non-fiction texts should include those closely related to the world of the child and extend to those which enable children to deepen an understanding of themselves and the world in which they live, eg. books about weather, wildlife, other countries, food, transport, the stars. Pupils should encounter an environment in which they are surrounded by books and other reading material presented in an attractive and inviting way. The reading material should include material which relates to the real world, such as labels, captions, notices, childrens newspapers, books of instructions, plans and maps, diagrams, computer printouts and visual display.

English National Curriculum: Programmes of Study

Criteria

Decisions about criteria for selecting books should be taken as a result of whole-staff discussion and an agreed consensus. Like language policies, such statements of criteria may need revising from time to time. Although criteria may be agreed, there may well be differing opinions on the application of criteria to particular books. Here, discussion with colleagues to explore different points of view is essential. Some criteria will be general and apply to all material. For instance, the images of the cultural groups represented should be considered critically and material should reflect a range of social, cultural and linguistic backgrounds and traditions. More specific criteria may apply to material chosen for particular purposes.

When choosing stories, make sure that there are

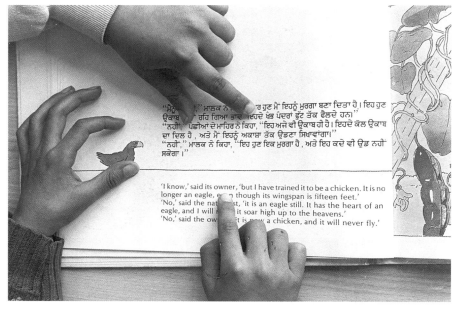

'I know,' said its owner, 'but I have trained it to be a chicken. It is no longer an eagle, even though its wingspan is fifteen feet.'
'No,' said the naturalist, 'it is an eagle still. It has the heart of an eagle, and I will make it soar high up to the heavens.'
'No,' said the owner, 'it is now a chicken, and it will never fly.'

many different kinds of stories. The range should include books which reflect children's backgrounds and experiences, those which extend such experience and provide insights into other lives, and those which go beyond it into fantasy, science fiction, folk tale, fairy tale, myth and legend. Look for well written texts, which are multilayered and can be read and reread with enjoyment.

When choosing dual language books where the conventions of the written language are different from those of English, for example reading from the back to the front of the book, it is better to have parallel versions in two books rather than presenting the book in an inappropriate form. This is again a matter for staff discussion and the particular circumstances of the school. In a school where there are no speakers of languages other than English, some dual language books introduce the children to ideas of linguistic diversity and prepare them for learning a second language.

With information books, look for books written if possible by experts enthusiastic and knowledgeable in their field, books which will enthuse the reader. They should be accurate and up-to-date. Where appropriate they should contain an index and/or table of contents, strong illustrations which add to the information in the text, and a glossary. The selection should include books that might be found in home or workplace outside the school, e.g. adult reference books.

The choice should also include books that reflect children's own interests' particularly for those children who show little apparent interest in reading. A book which deals with a hobby pursued in out-of-school time can provide the vital nudge towards wider reading. Other subject coverage can be helped by referring to whole-staff discussions on topics and to National Curriculum requirements.

Access to books for children with disabilities

Teachers need to inform themselves about any disabilities that affect a child's language and literacy. *The Primary Language Record* gives space for this information to be recorded, together with the source and date of the information. Each child has a range of individual needs, which will be affected by the nature of her/his disabilities. All children need access to books, and there are many ways in which provision can be made to offer access for disabled children. For example:

- Braille books for those blind children who read braille e.g. *Rolly goes exploring* (P.Newth Philomel, 1981) and three others in the series. Books with braille translations can be loaned from Clearvision (Linden Lodge School, 61 Princes Way, London SW19 6JB).

- Books with large clear print, books with collage pictures (either published or made by the children), books with pictures that have "sound effects" (e.g. that rattle or

squeak) can all help blind and partially sighted children gain access to books.

- Taped stories provide access to books for all children, particularly those who are blind or partially sighted.

- Videos of signed stories e.g. *Sign a Story* (Grampian TV, Queens Cross, Aberdeen) give real access to book language for deaf children who use Sign Language. It is important for deaf children to have access to books in their first language, as it is for all bilingual children. There are also a few books which include pictures of signs alongside the written text e.g. *Where's Spot?* and *Spot goes to school* E. Hill National Deaf Children's Society; and ABC books with finger-spelled letters and signs: *Animals* (Franklin Watts, 1988)

- Books on computer allow independent access for those children who have difficulty with the physical manipulation of

Where's Spot?

Eric Hill

Book suppliers

Where the school runs a school bookshop, the supplier will be bringing in stock. This can provide ideas and supply the school's own collections. Such suppliers, whether regional companies or local bookshops, can be a real help. In London, for example, Helen Paibo of the Children's Bookshop in Fortis Green Road, or, in Sevenoaks, Liz George of Another Tale Bookshop bring more than usual expertise to their advice to teachers. Outside London, Sonia Benster of the Children's Bookshop in Lindley, Huddersfield, and Madeline Lindley of Oldham are similarly well qualified and enthusiastic. Of the larger suppliers, Morley Books in London, Books for Students in Warwickshire and Woodfield & Stanley in Huddersfield – among many others – have a long tradition of supplying schools, and provide large display collections for teachers to browse among and buy from. They will also frequently provide additional services such as protective plastic covers or lamination for paperbacks. Many will provide stock for Book Fairs when both teachers and parents as well as children can see new publications. Most will give 10% discount to schools that are regular customers. Some local suppliers and bookshops will leave boxes of new books, specially selected to requirements, in schools for a few days for staff to talk over before buying.

A good annotated list of suppliers is included in the Children's Book Foundation's *Bookfax* (updated annually and full of information on children's books). Lists of local black and community bookshops may be available from LEA school library services or local teachers' centres. Second-hand bookshops can be a source of out of print bargains, a double gain.

Book clubs can be helpful; they offer special rates and frequent bargains. Puffin and Red House

book clubs are only two of many operating in schools and Letterbox Library offers help to a profession concerned about stereotypes of race, class and gender in children's literature. Dual language and community language books can be obtained through Heffers of Cambridge, a wholesaler that makes a point of stocking as many small publishers titles as possible. (This service was previously offered by Baker Books.)

Materials other than books in community languages are more difficult to find and specialist bookshops and suppliers such as – in London – Soma Books and Guanghwa, will need to be approached. Embassies and local community schools may be able to help and advise.

written pages. There are also machines available for magnifying print onto a computer screen for some blind and partially sighted children.

- When a teacher or other adult is reading a story or working with a group, deaf and partially hearing children need to be in the best position for them to lip-read or hear and partially sighted children need to be in the best position for them to see. This should be part of the routine in the class.

- Books in the classroom need to be physically accessible to all children. Children in wheelchairs or with other physical disabilities need to be able to reach all the books on offer so that they can make independent choices about which books to read.

- All classrooms should contain books which show disabled people as real characters,

not just as stereotypes. Rieser (Rieser & Mason, 1990) gives a list of recommended books, pointing out that

Good children's literature should help the readers discover the truth for themselves, rather than seek to convert the readers to a cause.

Hearing and sighted children will also enjoy exploring braille, finger-spelling and sign language in books, and will benefit from all the other ways of making books accessible too, so that sensitive provision for disabled children can be a natural part of the opportunities for all children.

3

Promotion

Enthusiasm for books is caught, not taught. Children – and adults – recommend favourite books to each other, and this desire to have others enjoy what we have enjoyed can be channelled and provided for. Informal talk about books and authors in class is the starting point for promoting reading. Teachers can structure opportunities for such talk and can introduce children to new books regularly by reading extracts from them in reading-aloud sessions. Children can be invited to introduce each other to books they have enjoyed, in small groups, as a class, or even in large school assemblies.

As well as this, children can be involved in many other promotional activies. They can design and make publicity material for new book exhibitions in the library, combining their publicity with material obtained from publishers, most of whom will send posters and book covers if asked. Exhibitions can be set up elsewhere in the school, in the entrance hall for example, to promote the school library and bookshop, or to draw attention to book events and the local library.

The school bookshop itself is a great promoter of books in the school, and is especially important in those areas where bookshops are few and far between. One teacher, writing about the setting up of the school bookshop, points out that research shows that successful readers:

- are book owners
- are read to frequently
- have favourite books, constantly reread.

Display

All books and materials need to be displayed attractively and conveniently. School library services can often advise on furniture and shelving. In the reading areas of the classroom, carpets and cushions give a warm, comfortable and welcoming feel. Picture books, propped open on every available surface, lighten and soften the look of any classroom. They need to be seen face on, particularly in paperback, but this is, admittedly, extravagant on shelf space. A kinderbox will take those which cannot be displayed, allowing browsers to leaf through them easily.

The listening area needs to be near electric points (battery use is possible but expensive). There should be room for up to four children. The use of headphones needs to be discussed; the quiet and concentration they provide needs to be balanced against their 'cutting off' effect.

Tapes need to be with the corresponding book, and Weston Wood's Hang Up System can help here. Their plastic bags containing book and tape can hang either from their free-standing metal hanging rails or from towel/wardrobe rails fixed by DIY methods. Pamphlet boxes or home-made card pouches fixed to the wall are another possibility. Arncliffe Publishing produce a large plastic hanging wallet for Big Books, which provides pockets for little books and cassettes. Taped stories, incidentally, can be commercially available, taped from radio, or recorded by teachers, parents or community helpers.

The presence of a bookshop on the school premises helps the first, and will foster the third of these points - while the second needs to be a part of school policy .

It is important that reading is seen to be a valued part of school life for everyone. Some schools make a point of having a quiet time every day when everyone, in every classroom, including the teachers, is reading. Storytime is of fundamental importance. This is when teachers can extend children's range as readers. Connections can be made with other books, other works by the same author or illustrator, other themes and ideas.

More promotional activities can include 'advertising campaigns' which can be mounted to publicise particular authors, illustrators or titles; the school or an individual class can choose a 'top ten', or (like the Times Educational Supplement Award) the best information book. This can be quite a prolonged affair, with all the classes voting, the final selection being left to a selection committee.

Some schools use assembly to promote books – a 'Critics Forum' reviewing new books for example, or readings from new or favourite books. Reviews can also feature in a library news sheet or magazine, or a parents' newsletter.

Children can help to make 'starter tapes' to go in the listening corner, for readers looking for suggestions for what to read next. These could have a brief description of the book, one or two responses by readers, and an excerpt or two – perhaps the first chapter. The ILEA project

'Hooked on Books' could prove a useful model here. Apart from the book (published by Harcourt, Brace, Jovanovich) which has dozens of well annotated lists of books for nine to eleven year olds, the video (from Educational Media International) features some of the books, promoting them in many different forms – dramatisation, excerpts, children talking about the stories, and so on.

Book events of one kind or another give a real boost to the level of enthusiasm and interest in books. These can be day long Book Fairs, or Book Weeks or Fortnights. There can be Poetry Weeks, Storytelling Weeks, Information Book Weeks or Picture Book Weeks. When such events are a new venture, it is comforting to know that help is available in organising them. Some suppliers will help in actually organising the event. The Children's Book Foundation provides all sorts of information, advice and ideas to do with children's books and book events. In addition, its publication *Bookfax* includes the 'Author Directory', which lists those writers and illustrators who are willing to work in schools or participate in book weeks. There will be expenses in connection with this, and financial help can sometimes be obtained from the regional arts associations. Sometimes writers can be asked back to schools for more than one isolated session. Two such visits can be productive, but it is possible for a longer lasting relationship to be established which will bring the writer into the school on a regular basis. For information on Writers in Residence contact the local arts association.

Publications to help with Book Events

Book Week Handbook
Obtainable from Children's Book Foundation, Book House, 45, East Hill, London SW18 2QZ
Free to members, £1.25 to non-members. Geared to Children's Book Week run by CBF (yearly in October) and celebrated by schools and children's libraries all over the country. Also useful as a source of ideas for planning, activities and general information for book events anywhere, anytime. Just before October, the CBF mailing to members includes a Book Week Pack, full of information.

How to Organise a Children's Book Fair
Free of charge from: Book Marketing Council, 19, Bedford Square, London WC1B 3HJ
As this comes from a publishers' organisation it is particularly good on approaching publishers and on what they can offer. Includes three accounts, from a school, a bookshop and a book group, giving personal experiences of 'book fairs we have known'.

Organising a Book Event
Available free from the Poetry Library, Level 5 Red side, Royal Festival Hall, London SE1 8XX
A useful duplicated handout included in the Poetry Library's *Teachers' Information Pack*.

Classroom activities for Book Weeks
Available free from Puffin Book Club, 27, Wrights Lane, London W8 5TZ
This is what its title implies, and covers book making, using different media (including computers) for telling stories, making props, and games.

For other storage ideas, Creswell's catalogue is good browsing material for items that can be adapted or improvised if money is not available.

Small collections within the classroom can be placed in plastic baskets, which both house and display them. Remember that books often belong to more than one category, and you may want to change them. Such collections could include:

> Books we know well
> New books
> Quick reads
> Longer reads
> Favourite songs
> Sets for shared reading
>
> Various genres such as:
> Alphabet books
> Rhymes and poems
> Folk and fairy tales
> Animal stories
> Humorous stories
> Information books
> Books in two languages
> Books by particular authors and illustrators
>
> Special collections such as:
> Books about tadpoles
> Books about monsters

Most areas, baskets, displays, shelves, will need clear labels, which again contribute to the reading environment.

4 Information books

For children to become fully literate in our society they need to be able to read fiction *and* information books, and texts in a wide range of media.

From the start, information books and texts need to be part of the learning to read process. Helping children to discover how they can learn *through* reading, both in the early stages and as they become more experienced readers, is an important part of this.

Far too frequently, reading for information is narrowly conceived in terms of 'study skills' or 'retrieval skills'. The practical classroom approaches suggested in this section may be helpful to teachers as part of a broader and more systematic approach to supporting children's use of information texts in the classroom.

The introduction of the National Curriculum has brought with it the publication of vast quantities of information books aimed at the need to address the 'content' of the NC, particularly in Science, Geography and History. The quality of information, language, design and layout, are criteria worth considering when selecting information books for the school or classroom.

Learning to read and reading to learn

In school, most children are introduced to the world of books and literacy through stories, rhymes and songs. Information books, too, can play an important role in the learning to read process. By sharing information texts and talking about the ideas and worlds they contain, children can become familiar with the range of material available to them. Having opportunities to read and discuss information texts (instructions, arguments, maps and charts) enables children to read in ways that are important for learning across the curriculum.

Information books can help inexperienced readers; pictures, diagrams, captions and photographs can all support the reading of a 'difficult' text. Many small- and large-scale studies have suggested that boys often display a preference for reading information books. Research findings also show that many more boys than girls underachieve as readers. Though the reasons for this are complex, it may be that paying increased attention to the reading aloud, discussion and shared reading of information books, will enable more boys to become hooked on reading and books.

Working with groups of children or with the whole class, teachers can begin to provide a model of development which will involve:

- finding out what children already know
- helping them to browse through books
- demonstrating how to go about finding information and how to present it
- organising the classroom so that children can share ideas, research and information (including information about how they found things out).

Children can be encouraged to jot down observations and questions in notebooks, diaries and journals as they go along. If information texts are part of the classroom from the beginnings of literacy, they can influence and extend the range of children's writing by showing the different ways in which information can be organised and presented.

Through drama, story and writing in role, contexts can be created where children have 'real' issues to investigate, and problems to resolve, using a variety of information sources. This is likely to involve children in interpreting maps, diagrams and other visual material such as photographs, newspapers and videos.

Through information books and texts, children can extend their capacity to reflect on what they have read and develop their powers as critical readers, by evaluating the accuracy of the information presented in texts and considering the purposes and audiences of a text.

Practical classroom approaches

- reading information books to children in whole class groups during 'storytime', or with smaller groups through shared reading activities shows that information books can be enjoyed in their own right instead of being used only in as resources for topics and research activities. Sharing and talking about information books with children is important for demonstrating what information books offer, how they work, and the variety of ways they can be read. Big books lend themselves to being worked with in this way.
- making overhead transparencies of information texts, photographs and other kinds of illustrations for the group to read and consider together.
- inviting children to raise their own questions when introducing a particular topic. A display could be set up where the books are surrounded by children's questions, alongside some of the information they have discovered.
- focusing on examples of information books written by the same author (eg David Macauley,

Aliki, Marc Brown, A and M Provenson) or those in the same series(e.g. *Stopwatch, Oxford Scientific Films, The Clue Books, Threads, and Fascinating Facts*). These might be read aloud and discussed together, looking at patterns of style and presentation.
- sharing examples of information texts (books, newspaper articles, diagrams) which deal with the same topic or offer conflicting interpretations of the same story. Considering together questions of presentation, viewpoint and interpretation, fact and fiction, and how to decide which sources are reliable and accurate.
- presenting information books which have been written and illustrated by the children, who can describe what prompted their interest, how they went about making the book, the decisions involved, what they learned in the process and what they would like to find out next.
- making taped versions of information books, where appropriate. These can be made available in the languages the children know by involving them, their parents, older children, and other members of the community in the recording.

Displaying information books

For children to have access to the information books available in the school and classroom it is important for the books to be clearly organised, labelled, and displayed. Displays are generally more meaningful and have a greater impact if they are linked with curriculum themes and issues under discussion, or support routines in the classroom. Information books can be displayed as part of an interest table where children are encouraged to 'look and do'. Alternatively books can form part of an exhibition of artefacts from a particular time or place.

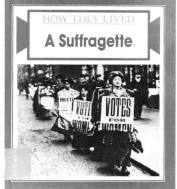

What makes a good information book

Information books need to be accurate, up to date and and should add to what children already know. Books are most successful when written by people who know and care about their subject. Good examples here are *The Eyewitness Guides*, written by experts in their field e.g. *Fossils* written by Paul Taylor in association with the Natural History Museum and *Cathedrals* by David Macauley. Books such as these stand in sharp contrast to the frequently anonymous voice of many information books, where complex concepts are often distilled into over-simplified language aimed at the 'younger reader', at the same time placing almost impossible demands on them.

The design of an information book should support children in their reading and browsing by the use of headings, inviting illustrations and photographs, clear and imaginative layout, introductory blurbs, summaries, bibliographies, index and contents pages. All of these can help children to tell at a glance whether a book is likely to help them with specific information they need or whether a book contains new kinds of information they might be interested in. The Eyewitness Guides (*Bird, Rock & Mineral, Skeleton*), The Stopwatch series (*Broad Bean, Snail*), The Amazing World Series (*Amazing Spiders, Amazing Poisonous Animals*) are well designed in terms of offering information to a wide range of readers through the creative use of photographs, diagrams, labels and captions, as well as text. Many information books which work well seem to offer, as part of their design and structure, a range of entry points.

Hardly any information books are currently available in community languages, and there are only a few in dual text form. As well as putting pressure on publishers, one way of remedying the situation is for children and adults to produce their own information books in a variety of languages, e.g. *The Greenhouse Effect* by Jill's class, Millfield's Infant School, published by Hackney Publishing Project, in Turkish and English editions.

Children can be drawn into the world of information books by picture books such as *The Man-Made Wonders of the World* by Dorothy Turner and pop-up books. *The Human Body* by Jonathan Miller and David Pelham or *Leonardo Da Vinci* by A. and M. Provensen are classroom favourites.

Biography and autobiography can highlight important cultural and historical issues. *The Afro-Bets Book of Black Heroes from A to Z: an introduction to Important Black Achievers* by Wade Hudson and VW Wesley, *A Suffragette,* by Ann Kramer from the 'How they Lived' series, and the *Time Life Library of Art* series, which combines lives of artists with prints of their pictures, provide excellent material for classroom research and discussions.

Some of the most successful books are those which provide starting points for explorations and experiments such as *Bread, Glass, Plastics* and *Wool* from the *Threads* series, *Light Fantastic* by Philip Watson ,which is full of science experiments to try out, and *Investigating Minibeasts* (Harcourt Brace Javinovitch) which comes in the form of a pack of laminated cards and a teachers' book.

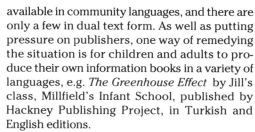

5 Reading media; using computers

These pages consider what is involved in reading media texts, and feature the two main technologies that are important to young children's developing literacies: television, which is such a key factor in visual literacy, and computers or word-processors.

*We see children entering the **universe** of discourse when they begin - very early nowadays - to watch television* Margaret Meek ***On Being Literate***

Picture and text

Most of the books that young children meet are picture books, in which pictures and text combine to tell the story. They often develop an extensive knowledge of the possible interrelationships between pictures and texts, and how these can affect meaning. (Some of these interrelationships are discussed in Judith Graham's *Pictures on the Page*). This very complex kind of 'reading' is always going on, and yet is rarely talked about – it would be helpful to discuss some of these issues openly in shared reading sessions with groups of children.

If children are encouraged to use picture *and* text to tell stories, as picture books, comics, cartoons, and television do, they can demonstrate some of this knowledge and put it into practice. Their story-making, or their story planning, can include pictures and picture sequences. The extra structure provided by pictures or picture sequencing may support their narratives. Later, they could learn how to tell a story visually and plan it through a storyboard.

In playing with pictures and texts (found in magazines, supplied by the teacher, or made by themselves) children draw on the tacit knowledge that they use all the time to read media texts, including adverts – perhaps the first reading lessons in this kind of literacy. They see how events can be presented from different angles and viewpoints, and how words can change the meaning of a picture. Games and investigations which involve children in this kind of activity bring in questions of bias, the images presented of people and places, and editing – how meanings can be altered or emphasised. One class of five-year-olds studied stereotyping by considering how princesses are traditionally presented in stories; the project, along with many other case studies, is reported in *Primary Media Education*, published by the British Film Institute.

Using still cameras, children can plan and photograph a story or news report they have composed as a group, and make up a text to go with the pictures. Groups can present their finished stories to each other and compare their presentations. Video cameras enable children to create even more ambitious texts, or to use their knowledge of TV styles of presentation to record school events – an outside broadcast of a sponsored walk, for instance, or a documentary about the preparations for the school play.

Media experience of this kind can lead to larger scale projects which set out to explore media techniques and apply them in new contexts.

Learning from television

Children find out a great deal about story from television, and they also learn how much the 'reader' of such stories has to fill in, and what certain visual conventions mean. They can bring this knowledge of narrative and its conventions to their work and their reading in school if encouraged to do so. Television is the supreme shared text in our society – experienced by most children. This is one clear finding from the *Primary Language Record* discussions with parents and with children. Another finding is that children's reading and writing is often TV-related - television can stimulate an interest in books, and inspire stories; it can be a stimulus to literacy.

Children are bound to bring their experience of television into the classroom; teachers can help them to use it positively. Children may choose to base their own fictions on television fictions they have seen (e.g. *Teenage Mutant Hero Turtles*) and it may support their stories to have this kind of framework, just as retelling or reworking traditional folk and fairy stories can help writing. TV is part of the culture of the home, and should be welcomed in the classroom; where it is, children may be ready to write more freely.

Software

The following programs may be useful in the classroom and are all available from ILECC, John Ruskin Street, London SE5 OPQ:

Allwrite (ILECC)
This is a multilingual word processing program which allows children to write in a wide range of languages. Alternative keyboards representing different scripts appear on the bottom half of the screen and can be operated by using the mouse. It was developed by ILECC Educational Computing Service and is obtainable from them at £50.00 for the first language and £30.00 for subsequent languages. A good account of this program at work is given in 'It Was Like Magic to Them!: Using Panjabi Allwrite with Early Years Children' in ***Primary Language: Extending the Curriculum with Computers*** (NCET 1991).

Write (Oxfordshire)
A general-purpose word processing program, allowing, as all such programs do, the creation and editing of text, with the end result a piece of writing that looks good.

Write On! (Software Production Associates)
A simple desktop publishing system, basically a word processing program which can include pictures made in *PaintSPA* or *NewSPAper*, as well as manipulating text

Caxton (Newman Software)
A simple, easy to use word-processing program designed for use by young children, producing high quality printouts (slowly) with large letter sizes in a range of 26 styles and fonts.

Animated Alphabet (Sherston Software)
A program using graphics in a series of 26 animated sequences to help children learn the letters of the alphabet and have fun in the process.

Developing Tray (ILECC)
The title derives from the photographers' developing tray where a latent image is gradually developed to form the finished photograph. This program offers a game where the hidden text is gradually developed by participants who guess missing letters, words, or phrases. The cues are those of context, syntax, grammar, punctuation, etc. This can be used by children of all ages.

Reading and word processing

Word processors are important tools for writers. They enable processes that used to be lengthy and cumbersome – like moving blocks of text around – to be carried out rapidly and easily. They can also make certain aspects of the writing process more visible, and perhaps more understandable. For instance, children soon see the need for scrolling text back to read what was written earlier – something that is a largely unconscious process, the reading back of one's own writing, is enlarged and becomes a subject for discussion.

Teachers find that children's writing, and therefore their reading, can benefit from them having access to word processors. For instance:

● children often write more than usual; the physical effort of writing is reduced by word-processing

● children who are reluctant writers (because of concerns about errors) often write much more willingly. They know their work can be edited and a correct final draft produced without exhausting effort

● able writers often see the possibilities offered by wordprocessing for working on their own texts, and begin to extend their practice of editing their work

● children can work together at the keyboard, collaborating over composition, and supporting each other with transcription

● children learning English benefit from being able to discuss and correct their work, and get better acquainted with English script and patterns of English spelling

● children generally begin to monitor their writing more carefully, and may spontaneously edit syntax that sounds awkward, and regularise spelling

● teachers can discuss children's texts with them on the screen, demonstrating how they can be changed about, and encouraging them to redraft a text, and edit what they have done for publication

● children's spelling often improves – they can see what they have written better, and match it with their visual memories of words

● children with poor handwriting are encouraged by being able to present their work in an attractive form

Because all of the above points support children's writing development and improve their understanding and control of written language, they also help their reading. While word-processing children are involved all the time in reading off the screen, testing their hypotheses about written language, and talking about texts.

A word processor is an enormously useful resource in a classroom where children's own writing is being published and becoming part of the reading stock. It enables texts to be well-produced and attractively presented. The use of different typefaces, and of different headings and layouts, enhances children's work and also reinforces the value of presentation. 'Writing workshop' approaches are helped by the use of a word–processor; drafting can be tedious if it has to be done by hand, but word-processing makes it a straightforward process.

Publishing children's writing greatly supports children's developing understanding of the uses of literacy. It encourages the development of the writer's sense of a reader, and the reader's sense that every text has been made by a real person. Desktop publishing programs extend the possibilities of classroom publishing still further.

6 Equal opportunities and reading

Provision for equal opportunities should be a thread that runs through all school policies, and it has been part of every section of this book. These pages emphasise particular issues that should be addressed in relation to equal opportunities and reading.

▌The content of books

School learning always needs to build on children's previous knowledge and experience, so the books provided in any classroom need to reflect the worlds that children know as well as introducing them to new worlds. This means that the bookstock in a classroom should include comics and catalogues alongside children's literature and information books, but it also means that children's books need to be sensitively chosen.

Many children's picture books are still set in an idealised world, where there is no poverty and where everyone lives in a white, middle-class nuclear family. Teachers will need to search for books which offer a wider world view, and where the experiences of working class people and people from a range of cultures are treated knowledgeably and seriously. All children need this wider world view, but for some children it has an added importance. If they never see themselves and their lives reflected in the books provided, they may reasonably conclude that reading is not for them.

It will be particularly important to consider the content of information books. Too often information books, without being overtly racist or sexist, simply leave out many areas of experience (e.g. black people's histories, women's achievements in science), so that they are made invisible.

Pictures are as important as text, if not more important, in conveying these messages. Only a minority of books move beyond stereotypes and tokenism in their representations of people and societies. Visually sophisticated children who have grown up with television are well accustomed to 'reading' pictures, even if they do not always articulate the meanings that they take from them, and their attitudes will be affected by the images that they encounter.

It can be helpful to discuss questions like these with children, and to ask them to notice how far different groups of people (e.g. disabled people) are included or ignored in the books available in the classroom, or in the newspapers and other texts they meet out of school. Older children can sometimes undertake straightforward content-analysis of texts and pictures, looking at the way that different cultural groups are portrayed, for instance, or considering how far books show women in traditional roles.

By talking with children about the authors of the books they read, and encouraging them to become authors themselves, teachers have also been able to demonstrate that the worlds described in texts have been created by particular people and reflect their views. Book-making, and meeting the authors of texts they have read are both activities that can help children to realise how publishing works, and enable them to adopt a more informed and critical approach to the books they meet.

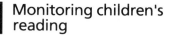
Equal opportunities policies will remain policies on paper if they are not regularly reviewed and if their effects are not evaluated. Monitoring children's progress is one way of seeing whether policies are working. This means looking at the progress of individuals and groups within the class and within the school through a process of monitoring.

Monitoring can be based on existing records. Lists of books that children have read will help teachers to review the choices that they are making, and to see which books seem to be supporting their progress. Individual reading records enable teachers to evaluate progress and check that particular children are not being overlooked. Records of bilingual children's reading in their first language, where they can be kept, provide fuller information about their overall literacy development.

Schools may also want to look at progress in a more formal way. *The Primary Language Record* reading scales provide a helpful way of monitoring progress at the level of the whole class. It will be positively helpful to consider the progress of groups within the class sometimes as part of such a monitoring exercise, in order to see whether equal opportunities seem to be making any difference to children's achievement (e.g. does improved book provision for boys seem to be reflected in any way in their progress as measured by the scales?).

Access to reading

Children who confidently see themselves as readers, or potential readers, are at a great advantage in learning to read. But frequently the 'literacy club' seems to be a club with a restricted membership, and reading is perceived as a white, middle-class activity, or as something that only girls are good at. How can we enable the majority of children to approach reading confidently?

Much of this book attempts to answer that question, either implicitly or explicitly. When schools make strong links with homes, review their book provision, or consider how they can give particular support to children with special needs, their aim is to give children better access to reading. Some approaches, however, seem particularly successful in affecting children's view of the reading process; here are three:

Demonstrating how reading works

Many current teaching approaches provide children with very clear demonstrations of how reading works. Shared reading and shared writing may be particularly helpful experiences for children who have not been read to a great deal, as they enable them to observe the process, and to join in a supported activity. Oral storytelling can enable children to make links between oral stories and those that are found in books, and between oral and written language. Retelling stories they have met, or making up their own versions, often as part of book-making, can be a key experience for children.

Demonstrating that adults are readers

Children must be able to identify with adult readers and writers around them and some schools deliberately provide role models for children. Where schools set aside a special time for everyone to read, one of their aims is to demonstrate to children the involvement of adults in the reading process. Inviting parents in to read with and to children, and involving fathers and men in reading activities, are also important ways of affecting children's ideas about reading. The storytapes provided in the classroom can be one way of making sure that children hear a range of adult voices reading. One powerful way to stimulate interest in reading is through book weeks and book events, which involve parents and other visitors. Inviting black writers and writers and storytellers from a range of cultures into school can influence the way children see reading.

Grouping children

Grouping may be an important way to support children's access to books. Children who share a first language may be able to help each other to read in that language or in English; girls working in small groups can support each other in reading unfamiliar information material; in some schools boys have benefited from reading together. Grouping can be a sensitive issue, but in classrooms where children are accustomed to working collaboratively it will be easier to vary the nature of the groups that children work in, and see what kind of situation gives them most support.

Equal opportunities: gender and reading

We know from many surveys that there are gender related differences in attainment in reading. Boys read less than girls, do less well in reading assessments, and are more frequently referred for reading help.

Despite these important facts, little in-depth research into gender and reading has been done. Much of what exists is classroom-based research carried out by classroom teachers in their spare time or through short-term projects. Valuable studies have included Julia Hodgeon's work in Cleveland nursery schools, and Pip Osmont's report for the Equal Opportunities Inspectorate of the ILEA.

Studies find that girls in primary schools choose to spend more time in reading. In the nurseries Julia Hodgeon observed, girls and women teachers often chose to read in the book area, while boys played in other parts of the classroom. Girls therefore have more experience of reading and books.

They are also more satisfied with the books available in the classroom, while boys would sometimes like other books, such as the comic books and annuals they read at home, to be provided. In general boys read more non-fiction by choice than girls do; if the information book stock is inadequate, or information reading is not given sufficient emphasis they may lose out. The books that are available may tend to present women and men in stereotyped roles, and rarely show boys as readers.

But the major finding of most research is that girls and boys identify strongly with the women and men around them from very early on, and model themselves on the adult behaviour they see. Adults may encourage children in this self-stereotyping. But even when adults do not encourage children to see reading books as a female activity, their behaviour may contradict what they say. Children rarely report seeing their fathers read anything but newspapers, though mothers are sometimes seen to be readers of books. Most primary teachers are women, and most home-school communication takes place between women teachers and mothers.

Julia Hodgeon, in a recent article in *Language Matters*, found that both teachers and parents were too willing to accept this state of affairs. She suggests there needs to be a 'deliberate sharing' of the problem of boys' underachievement with parents, as well as school policies to bring about change. Among the recommendations she makes are:

- the monitoring of children's reading progress (eg with the Primary Language Record reading scales) to see if there are marked differences in the attainment of boys and girls

- the involvement of more males - older boys, male teachers, fathers and male visitors - in reading activities in the classroom

- the involvement of fathers in parent-teacher discussions and home-school reading schemes.

- careful selection of texts that will appeal to all children, and will include books they read themselves at home, such as media-related fictions, comic and graphic books; the encouragement of reading in other contexts (e.g. word-processing and computer programmes)

- A careful balancing of fiction and non-fiction in the books presented and made available to children

- overt support for, and discussions with, boys, to foster independence in reading

- the making explicit of these concerns with parents, teachers and children, so that they can be directly addressed

Some of these changes would also benefit girls, whose reading of information texts needs to be particularly well supported, as they might not choose to read independently in this area. Much reading later in their school lives will depend on an ability to read a wider range of texts, and to use information material confidently.

Language variety

Some people mistakenly believe that children need to speak Standard English in order to learn to read it. This is not the case, and miscues in reading that are a result of children's dialects need not be a cause for anxiety. The accent or dialect that people use in their everyday speech is an important part of their identity, and an acceptance of children's home dialect helps to make clear that children will not be ignored or misunderstood because of the way they speak. Schools can demonstrate their acceptance of children's home languages in different ways:

Writing down young children's actual words
When teachers are acting as scribes for young children, it will be helpful for them to write down what they actually say rather than "translating" it into Standard English, particularly in the early stages of reading and writing. This will help children when they come to read back their dictated texts.

Focus on reading for meaning
Children who internalise the meaning from the written text and then say it in their own dialect are making sense of the text. Accuracy in reading is obviously important, but if the teacher, or other listener, interrupts too often to criticise a child's speech, the child will learn that the way s/he reads aloud is more important than the meaning of the text.

Books that use dialect
Some books use dialects in a written form and where possible children should have access to books that use their own dialects. To see a home language written down in this way can influence children's view of books and reading. An eight-year old boy whose family come from Jamaica, became thoroughly involved in reading *Caribbean folk tales and legends* aloud to his teacher. "I like reading Jamaican stories with real Jamaican words because they're like me."

Taped stories can reflect linguistic diversity
Some schools have a policy of encouraging parents, helpers and the children themselves to read stories onto tape so that they can build up a collection of taped stories, poems and plays that reflect the linguistic diversity in their own community. This helps to get across the important message that reading is for everyone.

Talk explicitly about dialects and languages
Children are aware of language and dialect differences at a very early age; they naturally alter their speech to fit different contexts. They may therefore be interested in, and able to discuss, the differences between different ways of speaking, and between spoken and written language. One of these differences is that, generally, Standard English is used in writing.

Access to Standard English
The National Curriculum includes the requirement that children should 'begin to use the structures of written Standard English and begin to use some sentence structures different from those of speech' in Level 4 of the Writing Attainment Target. Children who have grown well acquainted with the structures and patterns of Standard written English from their reading should have begun to use these structures and to write 'book language' well before this stage, and in general reading will be a major route to Standard English for most children. It will be important to discuss the status and use of Standard English with children, and reading will offer a good context for this discussion.

Faustin Charles' collection of Caribbean, African and Afro – American nursery rhymes and songs.

Me Granny old
Me Granny wise
stories shine like a moon
from inside she eyes
John Agard's poems from
Carribean proverbs

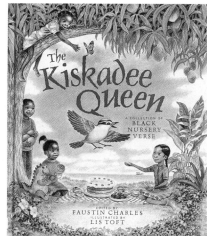

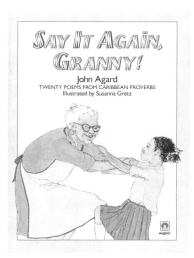

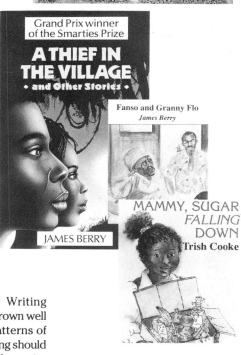

Culture Waves audiotapes(see booklist) are now available to accompany James Berry's *A Thief in the Village* and some other books by Caribbean and black British writers.

7 Supporting biliteracy

Although the focus of the English National Curriculum is on bilingual children's development as readers in English, there is evidence from classroom practice and from research that bilingual children will be helped as readers when all their home or community languages are valued and promoted in the classroom. The validation survey of the *Primary Language Record* Reading Scale 2 carried out by the ILEA Research and Statistics Branch found that 'fully fluent bilingual pupils were the most experienced readers of all.' This strengthens the view that continuing support for children's first language(s) is important even when children are fluent in English. Teachers have developed ways of doing this, and their practice has been built up over years of experience of working with bilingual children. The kind of good practice described elsewhere in this book provides a very supportive framework for working with bilingual children; here we describe particular aspects in more detail.

Cultural context

Having books in the classroom that reflect a variety of cultural contexts, including those that relate to the children's family backgrounds is of fundamental importance and can enable children to use knowledge that might otherwise be ignored. For example, a teacher planning a topic on 'Homes' included the children's wider experiences of the world, both their direct experience and the experience of their families. The children showed a keen interest in information books about buildings in different parts of the world; many of them had visited or lived in homes similar to those shown in the books. Careful planning of this kind will enable teachers to draw on the community served by the school for help with resourcing.

Books in home/community languages

Books written in children's home/community languages are an important resource for the classroom. Children can see that reading is not only about reading in English, but is also about reading in a language that they and their family speak. If children are learning to read in the 'first' language, or are already literate in that language, it is important that they are encouraged to read to their teachers and show what they can do. Books in home/community languages can be taken home by children for their parents or other adults to read with them There is a place both for books written only in home/community languages and for dual language texts (which can enable comparisons to be made between languages and writing systems).

Importance of listening

Children who are inexperienced users of English need lots of opportunities to hear stories, poems and information books read aloud. If a child's parents are not literate in English this will be even more important. Listening is a major means of learning for all children, and bilingual children particularly need the experience of hearing and becoming familiar with written English, which is in many respects different from spoken English.

Many classrooms have listening areas, where children can listen to taped stories, produced either commercially or by the children themselves. For bilingual children this can be a very valuable resource. Listening to stories, poems or songs in English will help them to hear the rhythms of written language and to learn texts in the early stages of reading. In addition, being able to listen to stories in their home language will give children access to stories and ideas which may not be yet available to them through English, and will support their literacy in that language.

Children making their own books

Many teachers offer lots of opportunities for children to make books in their home languages. This can involve bilingual support teachers, where they are available. In other situations teachers have asked parents for help. This has proved a good way to encourage parental involvement, and it puts bilingual parents in the position of experts.

As well as writing stories, some of which may be based on retellings of favourite stories, or on the work of published authors, children can produce information books in different areas of the curriculum. Some schools have published their own books in a variety of languages. *The Greenhouse Effect* published by Millfields Infants School in Hackney, is available in Turkish and in English.

Exploring stories through real objects and through role play

Where children are inexperienced with English, real objects, puppets and role play can be very useful ways into understanding stories. One teacher organised a display of taps, plugs, pipes and some plumbing tools when the class were involved with the story of 'Mrs. Plug the Plumber.' Another class used puppets to create their own stories, which were acted out for the rest of the class. Drama and role play can help to bring texts to life; dramatising a known text can support children's understanding of the story and enable them to use language they are learning from books.

Working collaboratively

Where children are given the opportunity to work collaboratively they can learn a lot from each other. Children naturally alter the language they use depending on the context, so bilingual children may choose to work either in English or in their home language depending on the group they are working with. It will be important to ensure that they have ample experience of working in both kinds of situation.

This kind of collaboration can be extended across different year groups. In one school a Year 4 class regularly visited the Reception class in order to read with the children in that class. Some Gujerati speaking older children were asked by the class teacher to spend time with the Gujerati speaking Reception class children. They read with them and told them stories in Gujerati as well as in English. They were able to give the class teacher more information about the children's literacy in their home language than she had previously known from communicating with them through English. All the children were enabled to use and extend their first language through this work.

Working with parents

The key role of parents in supporting their children's reading development has been recognised increasingly by teachers, educationalists and researchers. This has been reflected in schools by the formation of home-school links for reading, frequently known as PACT (Parents and Children and Teachers). In many schools, things have been taken a stage further: parents are asked to contribute to children's records in order to share their knowledge of their child's development, are sytematically informed about school reading policy, and are involved in reading in the school and in the classroom. We look at the ways some schools have approached these issues under the following headings:

● listening to parents
● encouraging parents to join in with reading in school
● informing and involving parents
● parents reading with children at home
● parents' involvement with reading in school

Listening to parents

The Primary Language Record parent conferences, in which parents' views are entered on to the child's record , provide useful opportunities for parents and teachers to discuss children's reading and literacy experiences. Schools not using the *Primary Language Record* can adopt similar principles: asking parents for information about the child's early literacy experiences including favourite books and TV programmes; finding out about languages spoken, read and written at home; the child's favourite kinds of reading (comics, newspapers, books from school or the library,

books from home etc.). Conferences also provide opportunites for teachers and parents to talk about a child's progress and for a teacher to answer any questions about what goes on with reading in the class. Hilary Minns' book *Read it to me now* shows the enormous range of influences on children's pre-school literacy development through a number of detailed case studies.

Parents should be able to feel that they can come into school and discuss their children's reading either informally or at a particular time set aside by the class teacher or the school.

Part A To be completed during the Autumn Term

A1 Record of discussion between child's parent(s) and class teacher *(Handbook pages 12-13)*

He likes reading. Every night he reads to his sister. He likes maths. Sometimes on a Friday or Saturday he helps in the shop and likes to count the money. He enjoys watching cartoons. Every Sunday he goes to Chinese school and learns to speak, read and write Cantonese. He's doing well at this school. Mum said she'll ask him to bring in his work to show. At home he fluctuates between speaking English and Cantonese, although if he had a choice he would choose English

Signed Parent(s) .... Teacher ....

Date 14 Oct

A2 Record of language/literacy conference with child *(Handbook pages 14-15)*

Encouraging parents to join in with reading in school

Reading with children
Some schools have a policy of inviting parents to stay and read to small groups of children during a time for reading first thing in the morning. Bilingual parents can be encouraged to tell or read stories in their first language. Often, most of the parents who stay and read are women, which can reinforce stereotypes about reading not being for boys. In this case, schools need to make the effort to encourage men to stay as well. Parents who read in school with children on a regular basis can also be encouraged to contribute to the class reading records.

Reading stories on to tape
Parents can be invited to read stories on to tape to boost the school stock of taped stories. This will provide an opportunity to explain the value of listening to stories. The school's equal opportunities policy would encourage bilingual parents to read in their first language as well as in English; men to read stories as well as women; those with non-standard accents to read in order to reflect the linguistic variation in the school community.

Making family books
Parents can be involved in making books for the school. Some schools have focused on bilingual parents writing books in their own language(s) and on parents writing about their own histories.

Other have involved parents in more extensive writing activities such as workshops and publishing. The National Writing Project in *Writing Partnerships (1): Home, School and Community* provides some helpful ideas for getting started.The Adult Literacy and Basic Skills Unit (ALBSU) funds a project in Devon which involves parents who lack confidence with their own literacy in courses such as 'Writing Stories for

▌Informing and involving parents

Informing parents about the school's reading policy is an important element in gaining their confidence and in enabling them to support their child's development most effectively.

- Meetings to inform parents about the school's approach to reading can include those for new parents as well as those which are part of a programme of meetings on aspects of the school's work. Schools can use meetings to advise parents on ways of supporting their children's reading and to stress the value of parents' unique knowledge of their own children's learning and literacy development åt home.

- Many schools publish their own pamphlet on reading which explains to parents the schools view of reading and explains how parents can help their children to become readers. Schools have also found the CLPE booklet *Read Read Read* very useful in answering parents' questions about reading and as a model for their own booklets.
  Leaflets can be put out from time to time to highlight aspects of school policy or in response to specific issues, e.g. the recent media debate on reading methods and reading standards.

- Videos (e.g. *Partners in Reading*, available from Hertsmedia), can be used as a focus for discussion in informal meetings with parents and some schools have made their own videos about reading.

- Loan materials can include: books from the class library which are taken home by children to read with their parents as part of the home/school reading policy; books about reading with children which some parents may like to read, e.g. *Read With Me*, Liz Waterland, *Learning to Read*, Margaret Meek, *The Read Aloud Handbook*, Jim Trelease, *Babies Need Books*, Dorothy Butler.

- Schools can provide booklists for children at different stages or reading development to help parents with choosing and buying books.

▌Useful resources:

- *Read with me*
  Liz Waterland, Thimble Press
  1988
- *Learning to Read*
  Margaret Meek
  Bodley Head
- *The Primary Language Record Handbook*
  CLPE 1989
  See Section A1 *Record of discussion between child's parent(s) and class teacher*
- *Read read read*
  CLPE 1984,
  available from CLPE
- *Read it to me now*
  Hilary Minns
  Virago
- *Partners in Reading*
  (video) available from
  Hertsmedia 0992 555872
- The National Writing Project
  Writing Partnerships (1): Home, School and Community
  NCC/Thomas Nelson
  1990
- *The Read Aloud Handbook*
  Jim Trelease Penguin Books
  1984
- *Babies Need Books*
  Dorothy Butler
  Penguin Books 1982

Parents reading with children

Home/school reading policies

Most schools encourage children to take books home, as teachers have become increasingly aware of the fact that parental involvement can contribute so much to children's success with reading. Schools who use the PACT scheme or other similar schemes often take the opportunity to have written dialogues with parents about a child's reading. These can take the form of note-books, cards, journals or logs. These dialogues provide opportunities for parents and teachers to talk about what happens at home and at school, to share worries and information.

Books taken home should reflect those normally available in the classroom. In this way parents can share in children's literacy experiences in school, and become aware of the kinds of books valued by the school. Home/school reading policies are most effective where:

- there is a clearly understood system for borrowing and returning books
- folders or zip bags are provided for books
- children keep some form of record of books they have taken out
- teachers address parents' worries and involve parents in exploring the different ways in which books can be shared.

Parents' involvement with reading in school

Exhibitions

Displays of children's own books written and published in the classroom, as well as exhibitions of children's writing, help to make explicit the processes of development involved in acquiring literacy and could be a major focus at a parents meeting or open evening. Displays of the kinds of published books used in the classroom could also be a useful part of an exhibition on reading.

Bookshops

Many schools run a bookshop for children and parents, either daily, weekly or as a special event perhaps once a term or as part of a parents' evening. This is a great opportunity for the school to involve parents in choosing books. Second-hand books, no longer wanted by children, or bought cheaply from charity shops, can be sold too, giving more opportunity for children to buy books. Children can be offered the chance to buy book stamps, which will gradually build up to the value of a book. Some book clubs and shops supply stamps, or the school can design their own.

Book Weeks

Having a book week is an enjoyable way of generating interest in and enthusiasm for books and reading. Parents can be invited to come in and listen to storytellers and authors talking about their books, as well as being invited to a book week assembly where classes can show the work they've been involved in - both reading books and writing their own.

Time and space for parents to read in school

A parents room, with its own small collection of books can be made available for use throughout the day.

13.9.88 'Meg and Mog'
Sarah read well, with some help from me. If she reads it again a few times she may feel more comfortable with harder words.

Sarah read this book several times over the last few days. Although she is trying very hard at the words she doesn't know, I still feel she is reading mostly from memory. I am quite concerned about this now as I feel she should be reading better than she is.

19.9.88 'The Fat Cat'
Sarah's reading well on her own, but needs a lot of encouragement as she seems to lack confidence. This is a long book, there are some hard words in it which I helped her with - making her look at the letters in the word etc. Hopefully, we can get her to build up her confidence and take it from there.

Sarah read this book over the past two days. She tried very hard at the words she didn't know, which I was very pleased about. I hope we can build her confidence together.

26.9.88 'Teddy goes shopping'
Sarah read some of the book with my help. It is a hard book which she will need help with.

Sarah and I read together, she also read the book with her big sister. She tried very hard with the words she didn't know and at least did try to make the sound of the first letter, which I was very pleased about. I hope she keeps it up. I was very impressed with her.

Extract from a home/school PACT journal which the dialogue between a teacher and the mother of a top infant (Y2) girl.

Some teachers have found it helpful to offer guidelines to support parents reading with children at home. One way of doing this is to include in the home/school book a range of ways in which a book can be read together, e.g. " I read this to my child. We talked about it." " We read the book together. My child took over the reading." Other teachers make different-coloured bookmarks to indicate ways in which they think a book can be shared, e.g. "Please read this book to me".

Parents may be worried when a child brings home the same book several times running. This may be because a particular book is playing an important role in a child's development or it may be because a child needs more help in choosing books to take home. A sharing of concerns helps to resolve issues like this, is informative for both teachers and parents and helps the child. Similarly, parents may be concerned that a book is 'too easy' or 'too hard'. It may be useful to discuss the importance of not seeing reading as a question of 'graded books' (this may be the parent's experience in fact), of valuing the need to read at different levels, and, with a book that is 'too hard', the value of reading a book aloud with a child.

A group of parents at Eveline Lowe School in Southwark have produced their own booklet *The 'Good Time' Reading Guide* which contains a set of cards with ideas for activities to support reading development. *Read Read Read* is a CLPE booklet for parents which schools can either give out or use as a model for developing their own.

Some schools are encouraging parents to start reading with their children long before reception class or nursery class. One school did this by having a *'Babypact'* scheme, where parents could borrow books for their pre-school children. The selection of books was permanently on display in the hall; it provided the focus for a parents area with armchairs, cushions and a carpet. The school also had a parents and toddler session each week from 3.00– 3.30 where they provided toys for the children and cups of tea for parents. This encouraged several parents into school and provided an opportunity for those parents already reading with their pre-school children to pass on the message to other parents.

The 'Good Time' Reading Guide by Parents at Eveline Lowe School(Southwark), Marlborough Grove London SE1 5JT

Helping your child with Reading and Writing
Sue Pidgeon, from the Puffin Book Club

9 Children with reading difficulties

A whole school approach

Schools should have guidelines for reviewing children's progress in reading at some point after children turn six, therefore allowing time for their needs to be supported. A helpful tool for reviewing progress of groups of children, in this way, alongside teachers' own records of individual children, is the *Primary Language Record 'Reading Scale 1: Becoming a reader'* (see *The Primary Language Record Handbook* p. 26) The scale is a descriptive, developmental one, which looks at children's progress as readers as they move from dependence to independence. Teachers should be alerted to the needs of children who remain on the 'Beginner reader' point of the scale, and for whom their ongoing records and observations show few signs of development. Significant exceptions here may be bilingual children who are learning to read in English and some summer-born children who may have had up to two terms less in school than some of their classmates.

A school needs to use all adults – primary helpers, parents, and others – as a reading resource for children. Class teachers should think of ways in which these adults can feed into the main class record on the child. Schools can prioritise extra teacher time to support children with reading difficulties in the classroom. They can also try to ensure access to bilingual support teachers to help those bilingual children who may be having reading difficulties in their first language; ideally, such support will have been available from the start.

Reading partners within the classroom can be one way of increasing opportunities for struggling readers to practise reading, as can partnerships that involve older readers with difficulties reading to younger, less experienced readers.

Observing children and identifying difficulties

Identifying difficulties involves looking *more closely and as broadly as possible* at the child as a reader. A teacher's detailed observations and samples will be of enormous help here. It may be useful to review the child's overall development under the headings of the *Primary Language Record* Learning Continuum:

Confidence and independence
In what contexts is the child motivated, confident as a reader, or as a learner? Are there favourite books? Does the child enjoy dictating her/his own books and stories? What use does the child make of opportunities for reading in the classroom? Does s/he browse, play at reading, read with others, alone, listen to story tapes, approach adults? Are there any contexts which adversely affect confidence and self-esteem? Are difficulties in reading reflected or not in other aspects of the child's learning - language development or other curriculum areas? Are there any sensory (primarily sight/hearing difficulties) which may affect development? Have you discussed these aspects with parents?

Experience
What experience of reading/literacy does the child bring to the classroom – from home, from other schools, classes and teachers? Have any experiences given unhelpful messages on what a reader does – what does the child think the process of reading is about? What languages does the child understand, speak, read, write? How can this information be used to support reading development in both their home language and in English? What experiences does the child have which can be built on to develop their enjoyment of reading?

Strategies
What strategies does the child use when reading? Information of this type is best built up over a period of time in a wide range of normal classroom contexts. The printed schedule on the *Primary Language Record* Reading Sample sheets provide useful guidelines:

- drawing on previous experience to make sense of book
- playing at reading
- using book language
- reading the pictures
- focusing on print (directionality, one-to-one correspondence, recognition of certain words)
- using semantic/syntactic/grapho-phonic cues
- predicting/self-correcting
- using several strategies or over-dependent on one

Schools may need to review their provision for children who have reading difficulties. In many cases, extra provision involves a narrowing of the curriculum: restricted work on phonics and impoverished texts. However, the working out of specific strategies should not be viewed simply in relation to tackling print: the provision of a rich reading curriculum is as important for the development of the child as a reader.

A school needs to involve parents at every level – informing them about the school reading policy, involving them in the classroom, setting up good home/school links for reading, sharing difficulties and successes.

Indications that a child is beginning to monitor her/his own reading – for example by self-correction – are particularly important signs of reading development.

Knowledge and understanding

What observations have you made about the child's knowledge of books and print? Can the child tell and retell stories orally? Does the child use the language of books in oral storying? In discussion with parents and from your own observation, does the child notice print in the environment? Does the child show interest in the letters of their own name, or family and class names? Can they read them? Do they remark on similarities in names and words? Can the child identify objects beginning with the same letter (as in I-Spy? Are there other indicators of a developing awareness of print?

Reflectiveness

How does the child view herself/himself as a reader? This may be observed both on more formal occasions where the child has an opportunity to discuss their reading (see Language and literacy conference – child and the teacher *PLR Handbook* pp 14-15), and also from reading and discussing with the child on a regular basis, observing how the child responds to texts, both individually and during shared reading sessions. Does the child bring her/his own experiences to a text?

Responding to individual needs

Using information from their observations, teachers can make decisions about what kinds of difficulties a child is experiencing and what kinds of support would be helpful. Observations, like those built up under the above headings of the *Primary Language Record* Learning Continuum, help to provide the very broad pictures of a child's language, learning and literacy development which are vital if the child's needs are to be addressed and their strengths utilised.

Motivation, confidence, self-esteem, previous experiences of reading at school and at home, experience of books and stories, and the reading environment in the school and classroom are as likely to be important factors in a child's difficulties as are the particular strategies a child uses to tackle print, or, in some cases, the particular medical, physical, sensory or learning difficulties which a child may have. Similarly, the provision of opportunities for success and experiences which encourage the child to become an independent learner are likely to be the determining factors in a child's development, rather than batteries of tests and highly specialised programmes which involve 'breaking down' the reading process.

The following categories may be helpful in deciding on provision for children experiencing different types of difficulty.

- slow to begin reading
- overdependent on print cues
- overdependent on meaning cues

(See Don Holdaway's chapter 'Developmental Learning and Diagnostic Teaching' in *The foundations of literacy* and Margaret Yatsevitch Phinney *Reading with the troubled reader* for extensive discussions of some of these points.)

Slow to begin reading
Strategies for supporting these children can include:
- much more experience of books and stories in a variety of groups and settings.
- use of big books where the matching of voice to word can become very explicit.
- modelling of reading behaviours by the teacher such as finger and voice pointing during reading aloud.
- increased opportunities for shared writing in small groups where the features of print– directionality, words, spaces, letters, names, as well as issues like rhyme and repetition can be focused on. *(Shared Reading, Shared Writing,* CLPE 1990 provides a helpful collection of articles which discuss these issues.)
- opportunities to dictate and make into books their own books and stories especially their own re-tellings of favourite books and well known stories. (See *Making Books Made Easy* by Olwyn Burgess for some basic techniques of book making in the classroom.)
- teachers can use children's names, family and class names, sweet labels and cartoon characters to make books that can help to develop awareness of print. Children can tick off their own class register on a daily basis.
- books, songs, poems and rhymes - from nursery rhymes to advertising jingles and pop songs – can be made into big books and sets of books for sharing.
- careful choice of texts which acknowledge the child's interests.

Most children overdepend on either print or meaning strategies in the early stages of reading as they develop the ability to orchestrate the various aspects of the reading process.

Occasionally , however, children may become

stuck and continue to be overdependent on either print cues or meaning cues. They may need support to move along. This does not necessarily imply specialised or separate activities. For example, an activity like book writing and publishing will be valuable to most children at all stages of reading for different reasons.

Overdependent on print cues

Readers in this group depend mainly on decoding strategies, and fail to realise that they can use their knowledge of the story, context, or language to predict words. Older readers of this type have often had a long history of 'scheme' books of the type in which decoding print has been the major method of reading. For these children, reading can become a slow, painful process, which is to be avoided if possible. Children may predict wildly, based on the look of words, and carry on despite the fact that the text no longer makes sense. Such children can be helped to develop reading by:

- using shared book writing to develop their understanding of how books and language work. Beginner writers can dictate their books and stories to an adult.
- listening and re-listening to favourite books and stories, ensuring that those with strong, rhythmic and lively texts are strongly represented. Taped stories and books are useful, as they provide opportunities for older readers to join in with stories in situations which are not too exposed.
- careful choice of texts which correspond to the child's interests, culture, family may help to make texts more meaningful
- cloze-type activities – blanking out the words in a text and encouraging the child to guess.
- a child's own books and stories can be photocopied, cut up into chunks and reassembled so that she develops an overview of a particular story.

Overdependent on meaning

These children may find it difficult to attend to print cues, using mainly their memory for books, stories and language to support their reading. Strategies which help to focus attention on print are:

- shared reading of books, including the modelling of finger and voice pointing, using strong rhythmic texts where it is easy to match voice to word.
- shared writing where all the features of print– letters, words, punctuation together with sound/letter correspondences and spoken /written word correspondences can be made explicit.
- cloze-type activities which use the first and possibly other letters as cues.
- writing their own books and stories and using these for reading material inevitably focuses attention on print in very important ways. Composing and typing up their own writing on a word processor further reinforces ideas about print.
- the use of word and letter games, e.g. I Spy and, Snap games using objects which begin with the same letter/sound.

Dyslexia

The term 'dyslexia' is commonly used to describe a child who is thought to have specific difficulties with reading and writing. The causes of such difficulties are fiercely debated by researchers (see Alec Webster and Christine McConnell *Children with Speech and Language Difficulties* and Margaret Yatsevitch Phinney *Reading with the troubled reader* for two discussions of recent research). However, many teachers, parents and children have found that labelling children's difficulties in this way can be unhelpful, as it tends to shift the focus on to a range of quasi-medical factors within the child, and away from the very wide range of issues which may be involved.

Factors affecting children with reading difficulties are extremely diverse, vary enormously from child to child and may include physiological, medical, sensory, emotional, and social factors as well as a whole number of issues such as home and school environment, motivation, personality and learning style. Similarly, provision to meet children's needs must take into account all of these, and should be based on the concept that learning to read is a complex orchestration of *many* different skills. Young and Tyre make the essential points in their book *Dyslexia or Illiteracy?*:

Instead of finding out what they can't do and giving them a hell of a lot of it, we need to find what they can do or want to do and give them the sense of achievement in doing it. It is even more dangerous if, in search of precision and clarity, we go on to exclude intellectual, emotional or socio-cultural factors.

Or, as Margaret Meek says in her book *On being literate.*

At present the research literature suggests that 'difficulty in reading' is the only common characteristic in all children described as dyslexic. The real cure is that they learn to read by experiencing success.

Children with statements of educational needs

For children whose reading difficulties are part of wider learning difficulties, formal assessment under the 1981 Education Act may be necessary, leading to a statement of educational need. This can result in the allocation of extra support within mainstream school, or to placement in a separate unit or school. Formal assessment is usually a lengthy process and good observational records will provide valuable support for discussion with parents, education psychologists and other agencies.

For children who already have statements of educational need, the strategies outlined above for assessing difficulties, strengths and strategies are as applicable as for non-statemented children. The degree of learning difficulty or disability a child has may mean that a child may move more slowly along the dependence to independence continuum, and that their needs have to be even more carefully assessed and met, but the process of acquiring the skill of reading remains the same.

It is important, moreover, that children's learning difficulties and disabilities should not be seen as a limiting factor in terms of expectation or provision. Children with language difficulties or with more profound learning difficulties may need a multi-sensory approach; visual and hearing factors will have to be addressed carefully.

However, in all these cases, the broadest view of the reading process and of strategies to support its development, will be most helpful to the child.

10 Keeping track of progress and development

The crucial importance of monitoring children's progress and development in literacy is generally acknowledged . Any kind of record-keeping system needs to be based on sound educational principles and on the collection of different kinds of evidence. It should be cumulative in nature, building up a picture of a child's learning, and clear in the way it communicates, not only to teachers but also to parents and children. Teachers' observations need to be structured, and record-keeping formats need to help them see what to look for. In the examples that follow it is apparent that teachers, parents and children all play a part in record-keeping. All contribute to the evidence by reflecting on the child's learning and evaluating progress and development. Record-keeping can be a collaborative process that contributes to better communication between all the partners in the process.

▌Structuring Observation

Information about a child's reading development can be gathered from several different sources, but is often more comprehensive if it is supported by a structured framework for recording observations. A helpful way to begin might be with the construction of a matrix showing the range of classroom contexts where a child meets stories, books and print. The contexts shown in the matrix reflect both the social and the cognitive aspects of a child's reading, in just the same way as the matrix in the *Primary Language Record* Talking and Listening Diary.

The matrix reflects the multi-faceted nature of reading in the classroom and identifies the range of contexts in which observations have been made. Teachers can see at a glance the emerging pattern of their observations. In the case of bilingual children, a third dimension to this matrix enables teachers to record the languages a child was observed to use while reading in these different contexts.

A matrix like this can serve as a structure for planning as well as a record; it demonstrates the range of opportunities for reading that can be provided in the classroom.

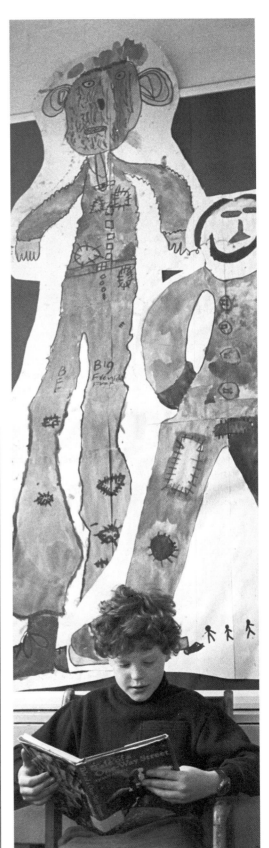

| READING CONTEXTS | SOCIAL CONTEXTS | | | | | |
	Alone	Pair/small group	Child and adult	Small group with adult	Large group with adult	Which language?
Listening to or telling stories						
Browsing and choosing books						
Reading aloud						
Reading silently						
Developing print awareness						
Discussing books and texts						
Using information books and texts						
Dramatic play and role-play						

Portfolio assessment in reading

If a record of a child's reading is not kept, how can teachers or anyone else discover her reading history? How can you deal intelligently with a class of children if you have no means of knowing what stories, what poems, what picture books and folk tales that group of children have experienced in the years before?

Aidan Chambers (1991)

For as long as we can all remember, it has been common policy for teachers to keep records of children's progress and development in reading. The content and quality of such records have varied; some have consisted of nothing more than a series of ticks beside the numbered books of a published reading scheme. Over the last few years, however, the policy of keeping portfolios of children's writing has led schools to consider how they can collect cumulative evidence of children's growth as readers.

This section provides a number of suggestions as to what might be in a child's reading portfolio. The list includes:

- diary of observations (teacher);
- language and literacy conferences (teacher and child);
- reading samples (teacher);
- reading journals or logs (teacher, parent and child, teacher and child, or child alone).

In addition it is useful for children to keep a list of the books they have read, and for some of these books to be reviewed for the information of their peers. Any list of books read can include material read at home as well as at school. For bilingual children this would be a valuable resource for ascertaining the breadth of their reading in more than one language.

Over the years, a rich and detailed reading history would emerge for each child. This would provide the kind of evidence that is needed to track children's progress and development as readers effectively.

Language and literacy conferences

A child's involvement in self-assessment can start in the nursery and develop throughout the primary phase. Inviting young children to consider their interests, their preferences and the range of their reading experiences can contribute to their learning and to teaching. Discussions like this may already take place informally, but on at least two occasions a year a child should have the chance to talk at more length with the teacher, to discuss experience, and to plan for the future.

With young children it is likely that the teacher will act as a scribe to record the discussion, but as children become more independent as writers there is no reason why they should not, with guidance, be responsible for writing their own reflections, as in this example.

"I think my reading has improved because I used to say "Mum what does this say?" but now I have got older I have started to sound them out. I am starting to read much more hard books like 50 pages in them, like The magic finger and things like that. When my mum is doing the washing up I say. Mum can you read to me and she said. go and sit in the front room and I will be in. And she comes in and reads to me and my mum thinks that my reading is improved so do I. I like to read hard books and I like the pictures better than the words."

S: An eight-year-old girl whose language is English

10

▌ Reading diaries

Diaries can be the most rewarding aspect of a recording system. They extend our knowledge of children's reading (and writing) development and bring to our attention new areas of literacy. They offer the most open and flexible form of record – but this can also make them hard to use initially, as they offer less structure for observation.

Teachers sometimes have doubts about what to include in diaries. A series of brief observational jottings seems unlikely to identify significant factors in development. However, those who have participated for a year or two in keeping diaries find that they are rich sources of information. Over

time, observers notice how individual children learn; patterns of learning become apparent, and key experiences can be identified. This helps teachers to decide how best to support children. The habit of observation developed by keeping diaries is also one of their major benefits.

In addition to the consideration of *what* to record, teachers often question *how often* they should record. The examples on this page show that there are many ways of keeping diaries. Examples range from a diary with several entries in a term to one with an occasional 'day in the life of the child as a reader'.

Ay: An eight-year-old girl whose languages are Turkish and English.

Jan	'I Hate my Teddy Bear' – uses grapho-phonics mostly. Knows how to use voice e.g capitals mean shouting. Is best reader at Assembly !
March 2	'Monkey and Croc' – I chose this to see what her strategies are. Uses grapho-phonic only – doesn't pay much attention to meaning – just says what she thinks the words sounds like. Read this book repeatedly.
April 20	'Stanley and Rhoda' – read this every day for 2 weeks to me A, S, and P(the student).

This example is more like a reading sample than a diary entry; the teacher has focussed on Ay. reading aloud from a pre-selected book in order to identify her actual reading strategies. But for Ay. this kind of attention is particularly important. Her teacher noted in previous entries how Ay. seems to concentrate almost entirely on the

grapho-phonic analysis of words at the expense of making sense of the text. This pattern concerned the teacher and so she continued to make regular diary entries., recording specific teaching support, until she observed Ay.'s growing ability to use a wider range of cue systems.
.

R: A six–year–old girl whose languages are Sylheti, Bengali and English

21 June 9.00 a.m.
She began the day by reading a Bengali word and picture book with N. our primary helper (who is literate in Bengali) and a small group of other children. They were reading the letters from the Bengali alphabet and pronouncing words.
1.15 p.m.
After lunch R. read Copy Cat and Old Macdonald with her friend. They read the stories together each holding a copy of the book while sitting on the carpet. Then R. read Brown Bear, Brown Bear with some other friends, all reciting it together. A satisfied look on her face when she had finished !

In this instance R.'s teacher has chosen to keep a diary of observations on one child for a whole day. Two of the observations are reproduced here and they serve to show that R.'s development as a reader in two languages is being supported in the classroom. It is also possible to note the two dif-

ferent but equally important factors in R.'s learning : *what* she is learning and *with whom* this learning is taking place. This kind of diary provides a brief but illuminating picture of the curriculum in action.

Sept. 88	Reading for information: I can identify areas of text which can give her the info she needs - has just sorted out strategies for doing this i.e. Use of contents/indexing, then searching for relevant info
Jan. 89	Readily engages in discussions about the way in which the story unfolds in a plot - leads in discussion and takes the work seriously.
May 89	Only understands nuances of text/literary allusions with support, but takes it on readily when explained e.g puns

Je: An eleven-year-old girl whose language is English.

For some teachers diaries have provided a medium for recording leaps in a child's development. This example from the diary for an older child shows how the teacher chose, on this occasion, to play the role of spectator observing a group of children discussing some novels and short stories they had been sharing in the classroom. The teacher was able to highlight some of Je.'s achievements as a reader e.g. coming to understand the ways in which narrative operates. She could also observe how Je. uses talk for learning, and how she operates in group situations.

Sept '87	Reading fluently and thoroughly enjoys reading fiction. Has just finished reading Silver Sword by I. Serraillier and is at the moment unable to pick up another book to read because, "I'll never be able to follow that, it was so brilliant and it's still in my head!"
Oct '87	Is reading a varied diet of authors. Keeps own record of books read at home/school and always makes valid comments which I'm able to discuss with her. Last year she got very hooked on L.I. Wilder series. Has read information books about the oak tree and woodland life in general and has taken some home to read and work from in connection with class centre of interest. Uses 'contents'/'index' well.
Nov '87	Has dipped into the Wilder series once more – "I know these books. I can really feel a part of them" – the whole of the family is reading them. "I enjoy reading to myself. You can read quickly and sometimes I skip over words. I can be 2 people in a book." When J. reads aloud she cannot read quickly enough for herself – often chooses to read passages of favourite books to me – to her mum.

J: A nine-year-old girl whose language is English.

Over a period of a term J.'s teacher had made three detailed entries in the diary. She had gathered her information from discussions with J. and used these situations to offer guidance and plan future work.

From the diary it is possible not only to find evidence of J.'s achievements but also to gain insights into the kind of reader she is.

She is an avid reader:
thoroughly enjoys reading fiction. . . . Had read information books about the oak tree and woodland life in general and has taken some home to read and work from

She is a reflective reader:
Keeps own record of books read at home/school and always makes avid comments which I'm able to discuss with her: "I know these books (L.Wilder). I can really feel part of them. . . I can be two people in a book."

Has established preferences in books and reading:
Has just finished reading Silver Sword by I Serrailier and is at the moment unable to pick up another book to read. "I enjoy reading to myself, you can read quickly and sometimes I skip over words."

Enjoys revisiting favourite books:
Last year she got very hooked on L.I. Wilder series. . . has dipped into the Wilder series once more . . . often chooses to read passages of favourite books to me (the teacher) and to her mum.

105

▌Reading samples

A child's reading development can be assessed in a highly focussed way by taking *samples* of their reading discussion of a particular text. Sampling might take place about once a term with each child. A *Primary Language Record* reading sample can be based on an *informal assessment,* or it can be more formal and be based on a *miscue analysis* or a *running record.* These forms of assessment offer frameworks for identifying the ways in which children read aloud, how they draw on the available cueing systems, and the kinds of strategies they use in the process of reading. The sampling procedures can be further supported by a framework that offers teachers guidance on what to look for in a reader's development.

Mooncake	
known text	
informal assessment	
C. has complete confidence in himself as a 'good' reader. He takes risks and has no fear of making errors. He has total concent? on the text which he reads fluently and fast. C. probably prefers silent reading	
C. draws on many strategies when reading aloud. He re-reads and self corrects e.g. 'in the to' in a big circle'. His miscues are not attended to if gist of text is understood & his substitutions are close to text e.g. edged for 'attached' and cheeped for chirped (grapho phonic?)	
Understood and appreciated story. Knew that Bear had mistaken the snowy landscape for a moonscape.	
A fluent able reader who is able to gain meaning. He reads expressively & with appropriate phrasing.	

C: A Year 2 boy whose languages are Panjabi and English

A sample like this provides an illuminating picture of how C. read *Mooncake*, a known text, on this particular occasion. It also offers insights into the complex nature of reading. The teacher is able to consider both this child's attitude to reading and his learning style. It can be deduced from the sample that C. draws on many strategies when reading aloud and is willing to reflect on shades of meaning. This sample, as part of a broad record, will make a valuable contribution to the assessment of a child's reading progress.

Reading journals and reading logs

Journals can take different forms and involve different people. They allow children, teachers and parent(s) to reflect on the child's experiences of reading, sometimes through a written dialogue.

Reading journals in many schools relate to home school reading schemes, and provide a record of a child's reading at home with books chosen at school. This practice enables parents to be fully involved in their child's school learning. As children become more independent readers they may keep their own reading logs, some of which will be written dialogues with the teacher. Journals are a means of children discussing and reflecting on their own reading, with or without an audience.

This selection of examples shows the developing purposes of reading journals as a child becomes a more experienced and critical reader:

"I like Princess Smartypants because Prince Vertigo has to climb a tower because of his name"

"I like it too. Do you know the story of Rapunzel? It's one of my favourites."

"Whilst I think of it - seeing as you enjoy Terrible Tuesday so much, keep it in mind for a piece of shared writing. If you have a really terrible day, note it down, you might be able to write –
– Terrible Wednesday maybe? losing earrings! sewing the tablecloth!"

A: a Year 3 girl whose languagees are Panjabi and English

This first example shows a young reader commenting on why she liked reading a particular book. The point she makes is an interesting one; she obviously enjoys the pun. The teacher is playing an important role not simply by acknowledging the child's comments but by guiding her reading and by offering her new ways of making connections between her reading and writing experiences.

I enjoyed one Rich Rajah. I enjoyed one Rich Rajah because in Gujerati it was written in English as well.

The Gigantic Turnip I liked it so much that when turnip grow bigger.

K: a Year 3 girl whose languages are Gujerati and English

A young reader of the same age as in the first example but who is also bilingual. Her writing shows her developing competence in using the English language and her ability to explain that reading in Gujerati as well as in English is very important to her.

11.11.90 Dear Mrs V.

I read The Class that Went Wild. I am still reading about Joseph goes missing. now the police is there as well and are busy looking for him, every one is worried especially Cristian Joseph's sister. I am really enjoying it! I read 1 chapter on page 203. I wish I could read and read and read . . . . Do you really enjoy reading or is there something better you like doing. I love maths! Any way do you like picture books as well? I do. I like all kinds of books, exciting ones, easy ones reference books and so on. I wish I could read like you and put all the action in like you do I enjoy it when you read it makes the stories even better

S.

thats all for now.

Thankyou very much S. Yes I do like reading very much and I also enjoy reading aloud to the class. I always know if I'm doing well because everybody is following & listening to every word which is satisfying. I'm better some days than others however although I do try! I also like other things too including maths! Have you chosen your next book?

S: A ten-year-old girl whose languages are Panjabi and English

This is a very short extract from a ten-year-old's journal. It does, however, give an indication of the potential of a journal for supporting the teaching and learning of reading. S. talks about how she enjoys reading a wide range of books, and how the teacher reading aloud contributes to this interest and enjoyment. The child has time to reflect critically on her reading, and the teacher has opportunity to assess her progress, guide her development, and nurture her enthusiasm.

Reading scales

Though all children make progress in their own particular way, there are common elements in their growth as readers. Children who are at the early stages of learning to read move from dependence on others towards greater independence, where they are capable of reading those texts that interest them. As children become more competent readers, progress will be apparent not only from their increasing fluency and accuracy, but also from the ways in which their experience as readers in all areas of the curriculum is growing.

The need to be able to plot children's progress as readers on a continuum *from dependence to independence* led to the development of the first PLR reading scale. This scale was originally developed for use with top infant children, (Year 2) but can also be used with children in the first year of the junior school (Year 3). Occasionally it may also be appropriate to use it with older children whose development as readers is slower and still like that of a younger child.

The second reading scale is designed for use with older juniors (Years 4, 5 and 6). This scale describes the developing *experience* of readers in KS.2, and looks at the way that older children broaden and deepen their experience of reading many kinds of texts.

The scales describe the processes involved in becoming a competent and experienced reader. As well as being used to identify individual children's progress, they can be used to monitor whole classes of children of the same year group annually, or at particular transition points in their education, e.g. Reading Scale 1 can be used for all children at the end of K.S.1 This practice enables schools to obtain an overall picture of reading progress in the group and to evaluate their reading policy and practice in the light of the

Validation of the Reading Scales

Two validation surveys of the *Primary Language Record* reading scales were carried out by the Research and Statistics Branch in ILEA, prior to April 1990.

An early unpublished report concerning Reading Scale 1 was entitled *Pupil Achievement in Reading*. A range of information was sought from schools in respect of nearly 4,000 top infant children: age, sex and reading scale category of each child, and (for bilingual children) fluency in English. The findings were significant and led to the recognition that Reading Scale1 had obvious potential for assessing reading achievement. The survey also enabled comparisons to be made between age, sex,(see table) degree of fluency in English, and progress in reading.

Another validation survey, this time of Reading Scale 2, was published in March 1990: *Reading experience of pupils: Validation survey of Reading Scale 2 from the Primary Language Record* Research and Statistics Branch, ILEA March 1990). This survey adds more support to the use of reading scales as a valid measure of children's reading abilities. It also highlights further the relationships between age, sex and linguistic background, and children's reading development.

Though this book is mainly concerned with children learning to read, the main findings of this second survey are still of interest, as they could influence primary school policy and practice. They can be summarised as follows:

● Girls tended to be more experienced readers than boys.

● Those pupils least experienced in English were amongst the least experienced readers. Fully fluent bilingual pupils, however, were the most experienced readers of all.

● The age of the pupils was related to the levels of reading experience of the pupils in the sample. Older pupils performed better than those who were born towards the end of the academic year.

● Parental occupation was strongly related to the assessed reading experience of the pupils in the sample. On average, children of non-manual workers were the most experienced readers, whilst pupils with 'semi/unskilled' parental occupation tended to be the least experienced in reading.

In the final discussion the researchers have this to say:

The findings of this survey indicate that Reading Scale 2 provides a valid assessment of a pupil's experience in reading and that, as an element of the Primary Language Record, *it provides additional and more wide-ranging information on a pupil's progress in reading than* London Reading Test *results alone. It is also an important formative tool in indicating which pupils need additional help with reading and what sort of support is necessary.*

Percentage of primary pupils placed in each reading category by sex						
Reading category						
Sex	**Non-reader**	**Non-fluent reader**	**Moderately-fluent reader**	**Fluent reader**	**Exceptionally-fluent reader**	**No of pupils**
Boys	9.6	32.0	29.2	20.7	8.5	2,004
Girls	5.7	22.9	30.2	28.9	12.3	1,987

information they have gained.

For children who are learning to read in two or more languages it will be important, wherever possible, to record their development in all their languages. This can be done through the scales with the help of teachers who share the child's language. Tracking progress in this way may reveal new areas of competence.

The reading scales have other benefits. They support teachers' planning for the class and for individual children's progress. The scales contain clear implications for practice and for the kind of opportunities and experiences that need to be provided in classrooms. The scales also offer teachers a shared language for talking about reading with colleagues. Because the wording of the scales is largely jargon-free, they also provide an excellent basis for talking to parents about children's reading progress.

The London Reading Test score was found to be significantly related to the stages children were assigned to on Reading Scale 2. The research team identified one other significant finding. It suggested, "that sex, fluency in English and social class have less influence on a pupil's assessed stage on Reading Scale 2 than on LRT score." A statistical analysis showed that the percentage of variation in reading amongst the pupils was markedly different for these two forms of assessment. These findings are of great significance and imply a need for further studies to be undertaken.

In the Summer Term of 1991 another survey was carried out in which Karen Feeney and Paul Hann, on behalf of Lewisham Education Authority, set out to investigate children's level of performance at the end of Key Stage 1. (Survey of Reading Performance in Year 2, 1991, Lewisham Education). The survey looked at reading standards in relation to age, gender, ethnicity, bilingualism and economic situation, and assessed the validity of Reading Scale 1 as a measure of reading performance.

The survey showed that there was a high correlation between children's performance on Reading.Scale.1 and the Standard Assessment Task and Teacher Assessment levels. It also showed that summer born children did not achieve as well as their older peers. Like the Research and Statistics reports, it found that fully fluent bilingual children achieved a higher standard of performance than any other group. There were significant differences between boys' and girls' achievement: half the boys were either in the beginner reader or non-fluent(developing) reader categories while two-thirds of the girls were at least in the moderately fluent reader stage.

All this evidence seems to support the extensive potential of the Reading Scales for monitoring standards of reading in schools. Regular monitoring of this kind can enable teachers to respond to the needs of all children, and particularly to specific groups who are found to be under-achieving.

---

for chidren between the ages of six and eight

Becoming a reader: reading scale 1

DEPENDENCE

Beginner reader 1	Does not have enough successful strategies for tackling print independently. Relies on having another person read the text aloud. May still be unaware that text carries meaning.
Non-fluent reader 2	Tackling known and predictable texts with growing confidence but still needing support with new and unfamiliar ones. Growing ability to predict meanings and developing strategies to check predictions against other cues such as the illustrations and the print itself.
Moderately fluent reader 3	Well-launched on reading but still needing to return to a familiar range of texts. At the same time beginning to explore new kinds of texts independently. Beginning to read silently.
Fluent reader 4	A capable reader who now approaches familiar texts with confidence but still needs support with unfamiliar materials. Beginning to draw inferences from books and stories read independently. Chooses to read silently.
Exceptionally fluent reader 5	An avid and independent reader, who is making choices from a wide range of material. Able to appreciate nuances and subtleties in text.

INDEPENDENCE

---

for chidren between the ages of nine and eleven

Experience as a reader across the curriculum: reading scale 2

INEXPERIENCED

Inexperienced reader 1	Experience as a reader has been limited. Generally chooses to read very easy and familiar texts where illustrations play an important part. Has difficulty with any unfamiliar material and yet may be able to read own dictated texts confidently. Needs a great deal of support with the reading demands of the classroom. Over-dependent on one strategy when reading aloud; often reads word by word. Rarely chooses to read for pleasure.
Less experienced reader 2	Developing fluency as a reader and reading certain kinds of material with confidence. Usually chooses short books with simple narrative shapes and with illustrations and may read these silently; often re-reads favourite books. Reading for pleasure often includes comics and magazines. Needs help with the reading demands of the classroom and especially with using reference and information books.
Moderately experienced reader 3	A confident reader who feels at home with books. Generally reads silently and is developing stamina as a reader. Is able to read for longer periods and cope with more demanding texts, including children's novels. Willing to reflect on reading and often uses reading in own learning. Selects books independently and can use information books and materials for straightforward reference purposes, but still needs help with unfamiliar material, particularly non-narrative prose.
Experienced reader 4	A self-motivated, confident and experienced reader who may be pursuing particular interests through reading. Capable of tackling some demanding texts and can cope well with the reading of the curriculum. Reads thoughtfully and appreciates shades of meaning. Capable of locating and drawing on a variety of sources in order to research a topic independently.
Exceptionally experienced reader 5	An enthusiastic and reflective reader who has strong established tastes in fiction and/or non-fiction. Enjoys pursuing own reading interests independently. Can handle a wide range and variety of texts, including some adult material. Recognises that different kinds of texts require different styles of reading. Able to evaluate evidence drawn from a variety of information sources. Is developing critical awareness as a reader.

EXPERIENCED

One School's Reading Policy

Contents

1. Aims

For children:

From their earliest years to have high expectations of books as sources of enjoyment and information.

To appreciate that books are produced by authors, illustrators and publishers, and to develop opinions about the work of these people

To involve themselves in books that illuminate their experience, enrich their language and learning, and make them aware of worlds beyond the everyday.

To build their own collections of books, and to use the public library

To encounter books in a variety of languages

To develop an interest in books in their Heritage Languages, and where possible, to learn to read them

To develop from inexperienced readers who need support to independent readers who can and do read at different levels and for different purposes

2. Book areas

We arrange attractive, well-stocked book areas in every classroom so that from their first days in school, children can develop the habit of browsing amongst books and choosing for themselves the books they are interested in reading.

Our books are chosen for the quality of their text and illustrations. We buy books that will appeal to children and will in other ways support them as they learn to read. We try to avoid books that display prejudice, or stereotypes of race, gender, and class. We encourage children to be critical of the books they encounter.

Children have access to books from various genres, fiction and non-fiction, poetry, song books. Our books present various cultural backgrounds and we have books in various languages.

We arrange displays to promote enthusiasm and care for the classroom book stock, highlighting particular authors, illustrators, themes and genres. Children can be involved in planning, setting up and maintaining these displays.

Block loans from the school library and borough libraries can be used to supplement class book collections.

3. Reading heritage languages

In an ideal school, all children would learn to read the languages that are important in their lives. In our school children would read English alone, or with equal facility, English and another language - Gujarati, Panjabi, Portugese, Tamil, Turkish, Urdu.

In this environment, all our children would learn incidentally about the importance of reading to people all over the world, and about the various symbols that have been developed to represent language.

How close can we get to this in reality? At present Sikh children from junior classes learn Panjabi literacy for forty minutes a week with Miss B. Even these short sessions are welcomed by the children and their families. We should highlight the childrens' work in our classrooms and Sharing Assemblies, and arrange (in consultation with Miss B) for them to use what they learn.

Other bilingual children learn literacy from their parents and in community classes. We can create opportunities for them to share this experience in school.

Bilingual colleagues might help us to set other written languages alongside English in our displays and book areas. Children's families may also be prepared to help us with this.

Broad arguments for supporting bilingualism, and a summary of policy are reproduced in an appendix to this document.

4. Our knowledge of children's literature

It is vital that we get to know the books in our classroom (and beyond) so that we can guide children in their choices. Post-holders and other colleagues can assist, pointing to reviews and annotated booklists, but ultimately it is an important professional responsibility to read children's literature ourselves.

5. Teachers reading aloud

We read aloud up to three times daily for these reasons:

– to develop children's understanding and appreciation of written language
– to promote particular books from the class and school libraries and from Bookbase
– to build for inexperienced readers a repertoire of books that they know well and which support them as they learn to tackle print themselves
– to demonstrate useful strategies in reading.

We often involve children in critical discussions of authors' and illustrators' work, and encourage them to make links between what is read and their own experience.

6. Sustained reading times

The first half hour of every afternoon session is set aside for children to read silently or quietly. Profitable use of this time has to be established and monitored over a period of time with a new class: some children need guidance in choosing what to read at these times.

We use these sessions to observe children and listen to them reading aloud.

Younger children should aim at short but lengthening periods of reading to themselves.

7. Reading for different purposes

Children are involved, day to day, in reading a variety of materials for a range of different purposes. We look for opportunities to widen this range.

As children develop as readers we should encourage them to fit the way that they read to their purpose in reading.

Computer software related to reading is detailed in the bibliography.

8. Children reading aloud

There are two main purposes for children reading aloud:
  i   to entertain and inform others
  ii to read books that would be difficult to tackle unaided and which reveal their reading strategies to adults who can help.

Both kinds of reading aloud are important. The first might involve children in selecting and preparing readings for their audience, These are opportunities for children to share the pleasure reading gives them.

The second kind of reading aloud is potentially more stressful. It can take all our skill and sensitivity to judge when to take over the reading for a child, when to hold back, and when to prompt the use of one strategy or another. Whatever we do should help children to become keen, independent readers.

We must judge what issues it is useful to raise with a child immediately and what to note for our attention later. These judgements are based on our knowledge of how children develop as readers, and the stage in this developmental sequence each child has reached. Models of development are described in section 12.

Hearing children read makes great demands on time. We might pattern more substantial Reading Conferences with each child over greater intervals of time.

9. Parents and their child's reading

It is vital that we communicate to parents our understandings of the way children learn to read, and our policies on reading. We can learn a great deal from parents about their children's interests outside school (including their heritage languages) and about wider interests and experiences which may be extended through reading in school.

The PACT scheme is one means to sharing children's reading development with their parents. Children choose books from class and school libraries. These are noted by class teachers, and taken home in a folder with a booklet which parents and teachers can use to make comments on a childs reading.

Checking the PACT note-books, and responding to parents' comments can take up to forty minutes a day. We must let parents know the kind of intervals they can expect us to write at, otherwise they may not feel it worthwhile writing themselves.

Parents comments may reveal anxieties about their child's progress, or other causes for concern (sometimes inappropriate ways of working with their child) which we should arrange to discuss with them as soon as possible.

Parents should feel that they can arrange to discuss their child's progress with us at any mutually convenient time. The language post-holder and the head may be involved in this.

It may be useful to meet groups of parents from time to time to discuss the PACT scheme. The language post-holder can assist.

10. Bookbase

Having books of their own is an important influence on children's development as readers. Bookbase (the school bookshop) gives children and their parents the opportunity to buy quality books, and to discuss choices of books with teachers.

Bookbase runs all day every Friday. Teachers can arrange a time to take their class. There is a savings scheme for children. Class teachers make their own arrangements concerning the collection of money. Savings cards can be obtained from Mrs. V, who will also take Bookbase money at any time.

11. The school library
The library houses a collection of fiction , information books, charts and slide packs. Fiction is shelved according to author. Other books and resources are classified according to a simplified Dewey System and are colour coded.

Weekly sessions in the library are timetabled for each class so that children can borrow books and learn to locate and use all the resources housed there. Access for children at other times will depend on staffing arrangements.

There are games and other materials

available to teachers to develop children's library skills.

12. Developing reading

Useful models of children's development as readers are to be found in Liz Waterland's Reading Behaviour Development table from *Read With Me*, and 'Reading Scales 1 and 2' from *Primary Language Record Handbook for Teachers*(CLPE)

13. Writing and reading

It is in the course of writing that young children can most actively develop their knowledge of written language. Much of the attention to details of print involved in traditional 'phonics' teaching can best be encouraged in work on writing.

14. Monitoring and recording

The *Primary Language Record* requires Samples of each child's reading to be described in the following terms:
Title of book or text: fiction or information: known or unknown.

  i Overall impression of the child's reading:
- confidence and degree of independence
- involvement in the book
- the way in which the child read aloud

  ii Strategies the child used when reading aloud:
- used illustrations (to retell the story or check guesses)
- used context to help work out meaning and see that reading made sense
- read in meaningful "chunks" (or word by word)
- used the structures of language to help work out meaning
- used knowledge of what words and letters look and sound like to help work out unknown word
- How child tackled unknown word; good guess? Waited to be told?
- used several strategies to get meaning from text, or depended heavily on one (e.g. phonic analysis)
- child self-corrected, seemed to be monitoring own reading

  iii Child's response to the books:
- personal response
- critical response (understanding, evaluating, appreciating wider meanings)

  iv What this sample shows about the child's development as a reader Experiences and support needed to further development.

These samples, and diary entries noting the extent of the child's reading, form the basis for a statement on the child's progress and development as a reader in these terms:
    The stage at which the child is operating (referring to Reading Fluency Scales - see *Primary Language Record Handbook* pp 26 & 27)
    the range, quantity and variety of reading in all areas of the curriculum
    the child's pleasure and involvement in story and reading, alone and with others
    the range of strategies used when reading and the child's ability to reflect on what is read.

It would be sensible to make our day to day notes on children's reading in these terms.

15. Standardised reading tests

There are helpful comments on the uses and drawbacks of standardised tests of reading in the *Thomas Report* paragraphs 2.92-97 & 2.246-248.

We use the *Gap Test* with junior classes late in the Summer term. The results give the Head an indication of the spread of performance in reading (as measured by the Test) across a year group. **Reading scores for individual children must be interpreted with great caution**. The *Primary Language Record* involves the collection of much more useful information about an individual child's strengths and weaknesses in reading which will guide teachers in promoting further progress.

16. Focussing on children's reading strategies

Procedures that can give us a detailed picture of the strategies a child is using to read include the Informal Inventory, Running Records, and Miscue Analysis. Learning to use these procedures develops our understanding of the processes involved in reading. It is likely that we will need to work on this together. References to detailed guidance are:

Informal Inventories
Independence in Reading
Don Holdaway   Appendix A
'Running Records' *The Early Detection of Reading Difficulties*
Marie Clay pp 93-94

Miscue Analysis   *Hearing Children Read*
Helen Arnold   Chap. 4

17. Children who find reading difficult

When children are failing to make progress in reading they should be brought to the attention of the Language post-holder and the Head. Support staff may be allocated to work with these children or to give the class teacher more time to do so.

(The *Primary Language Record* provides for all staff involved with a child to contribute observations and recommendations. There is a section for the outcome of any consultations with post-holders and the Head to be recorded.)

We thank Bannockburn School, London Borough of Greenwich, for allowing us to reprint this reading policy for the interest of other schools).

Bibliography

Children's books referred to in the text

The Afro-Bets book of black heroes from 'A to Z: an introduction to important black achievers', by Wade Hudson and V.W. Wesley.
Just Us Books (available from Africa Centre, King St., London WC2.

Ahhh! said Stork, by Gerald Rose.
Faber and Picturemac.

'Amazing World' series.
Dorling Kindersley.

Anansi and the alligator eggs; from Tales of the Caribbean told by Evan Jones,
Ginn.

Angry Arthur; by Hiawyn Oram.
Andersen and Picture Puffin.

Animals and four other titles; with finger spelled letters and signs.
Watts.

Are you my mother?, by P.D.Eastman.
Collins.

The Bird who was an elephant, by Aleph Kamal. Dual language versions also available.
Cambridge University Press.

Breakthrough to literacy,
Longman.

'Brent Young Writers' Series,
Brent Library Information Resources Centre

Bringing the rain to Kapiti Plain, by Verna Aardema. Picturemac.

Brown bear, brown bear, by Bill Martin.
H.Hamilton and Picture Lions.

Burglar Bill; by Allan and Janet Ahlberg.
Heinemann and Mammoth.

Calypso alphabet, by John Agard.
Collins

Caribbean folk tales and legends by Andrew Salkey.
Bogle L'Ouverture.

The Cat on the mat, by Brian Wildsmith.
Oxford University Press.

Cathedrals, by David Macauley.
Collins.

Changes, changes, by Pat Hutchins. Bodley Head.

'Clue Books' series.
Oxford University Press.

Come away from the water, Shirley, by John Burningham.
Cape and Picture Lions.

Come on into my tropical garden, by Grace Nicholls.
Black.

Copy cat, by Kathleen and D. Herson.
Simon & Schuster.

Curtis the hip hop cat, by Gini Wade.
Macmillan.

The Dark, dark tale, Various editions.

Dear Zoo, by Rod Campbell.
Picture Puffin. Dual language versions available from Ingham Yates.

Dinner time, pop-up book by Jan Pienkowski.
Orchard.

Don't forget the bacon, by Pat Hutchins. Bodley Head and Picture Puffins.

Dr. Seuss books, Collins.

Each peach pear plum, by Allan and Janet Ahlberg.
Picture Puffin.

'Eyewitness Guides' series.
Dorling Kindersley.

'Fascinating Facts' series.
Collins.

The Fat cat, by Jack Kent.
Picture Puffin.

Fossil, by Paul Taylor.
Dorling Kindersley

Funnybones, by Allan and Janet Ahlberg.
Heinemann and Mammoth.

Gargling with jelly, by Brian Patten.
Viking Kestrel and Picture Puffin.

The Greenhouse effect, by Jill's class at Millfields Infant School, Hackney Schools Publishing Project.

Guiness Book of records,
Guiness.

The Hobyahs, by Joseph Jacobs. Illustrated by Simon Stern.
Methuen.

How do I put it on?, by Shigeo Watanabe.
Bodley Head and Picture Puffin.

The Human Body, by Jonathan Miller and David Pelham.
Cape.

I want my potty, by Tony Ross.
Andersen and Picture Lions.

John Brown, Rose and the midnight cat; by Jenny Wagner.
Viking Kestrel and Picture Puffin.

John Burningham books,
Cape.

The Jolly Postman, by Janet and Allan Ahlberg.
Heinemann.

Journey with the Gods, by Linda Shanson and Anita Chowdry. Community language versions also available. Mantra.

Just like Daddy, by Frank Asch.
Carousel.

Kaleidoscope Boxes, Books for Students.

The Kiskadee Queen, ed. by Faustin Charles.
Blackie.

Leonardo Da Vinci, by A.and M. Provensen.
Hutchinson.

Light fantastic, by Philip Watson.
Walker.

Little red hen,
Various editions.

Look what I've got, by Anthony Browne.
Julia MacRae.

The Magic finger, by Roald Dahl. Harper Collins and Young Puffin.

Maisy goes swimming, by Lucy Cousins. Walker.

Mammy, Sugar Falling Down, by Trish Cooke. Hutchinson. Audiotape available from Culture Waves Ltd. (see Addresses).

Man-made wonders of the world, by Dorothy Turner.
Macmillan.

Maybe it's a tiger; by Kathleen Herson.
Picturemac.

Meg and Mog books, by Helen Nicoll and Jan Pienkowski.
Heinemann and Picture Puffin.

Mr. Archimedes' bath, by Pamela Allen.
Hamilton.

Mr. Gumpy's outing; by John Burningham.
Cape and Picture Puffin.

Mr. Magnolia, by Quentin Blake.
Cape and Picture Lions.

Mr. Rabbit and the lovely present, by Charlotte Zolotow.
Bodley Head.

Mrs. Plug the plumber; by Allan Ahlberg. Viking Kestrel and Puffin.

Mooncake, by Frank Asch.
Picture Corgi.

Mother gave a shout, poems by women and girls, by Morag Styles and Susanna Steele.
Black.

My cat likes to hide in boxes, by Eve Sutton.
Spindlewood and Picture Puffin.

My Class looks after Pets, (Bengali edition).
Watts.

Noisy Nora, by Rosemary Wells.
Collins and Picture Lions.

Not now, Bernard, by David McKee.
Andersen and Sparrow. Dual language versions available from Ingham Yates.

The Old woman and the rice thief, by Betsy Bang.
Hamilton.

One rich rajah, by Sheila Front. Dual language versions available.
Deutsch.

One, two, three and away,
Collins.

The Owl and the pussycat, by Edward Lear.
Various editions.

Oxford Readers,
Oxford University Press.

'Oxford Scientific Films' Series.
Deutsch.

Peter's chair, by Ezra Jack Keats.
Bodley Head and Red Fox.

Pinocchio, by Carlo Collodi.
Various editions.

Princess Smartypants, by
Babette Cole.
Hamilton and Picture Lions.

Reading with Rhythm,
Longman.

Rolly goes exploring, by
P.Newth.
Philomel.

Rosie's walk, by Pat Hutchins.
Bodley Head and Picture
Puffins.

Royal Road, Chatto & Windus.

Say it Again, Granny!, by John
Agard.
Methuen Magnet

Scripts of the world, by Susanne
Bukiet.
Mantra.

*Seasons of Splendour: tales,
myths and legends of India,* by
Madhur Jaffrey.
Pavilion.

Sign a story;
Grampian T.V.

Silly stories by Michael Rosen.
Kingfisher.

The Silver sword, by Ian
Serraillier.
Cape and Puffin books.

The Snowman, by Raymond
Briggs.
Hamilton and Picture Puffin.

*Speaking for ourselves and other
poems,* by Hiawyn Oram.
Methuen.

Spot books, by Eric Hill.
Heinemann and Picture Puffin.
Also National Deaf Children's
Society edition. Dual language
versions available from Heffers.

'Stopwatch' series, Black

A story, a story, an African tale;
by Gail Haley. Methuen.

Story Chest, Nelson.

A Strong and willing girl, by
Dorothy Edwards. Methuen
and Magnet.

A Suffragette, by Anne Kramer.
Wayland

*Tales of Uncle Remus; the
adventures of Brer Rabbit* as told
by Julius Lester.
Bodley Head.

Ten, nine, eight; by Molly Bang.
Julia MacRae and Picture Puffin.

Terrible Tuesday, by Hazel
Townson and Tony Ross.
Andersen and Beaver.

That's my Dad, by Ralph
Steadman.
Andersen and Arrow.

A Thief in the Village, by James
Berry. Hamish Hamilton and
Puffin. Audiotapes of stories
available from Culture Waves
Ltd. (see Addresses).

Three Billy goats gruff; Various
editions.

Three up a tree, by James
Marshall.
Black.

Titch, by Pat Hutchins.
Bodley Head and Picture Puffin.

Transformers annual, Marvel
Comics.

*The True story of the three little
pigs by A Wolf,* by Jon Scieszka.
Viking Kestrel.

The Very hungry caterpillar, by
Eric Carle.
Hamilton and Picture Puffin.

The Way things work, by David
Macaulay.
Dorling Kindersley.

Whatever next; by Jill Murphy.
Macmillan.

What's the time Mr. Wolf, by
Colin Hawkins.
Picture Lions.

When I dance, by James Berry.
Hamilton and Puffin.

Where the sidewalk ends, by
Shel Silverstein.
Cape.

Where the wild things are, by
Maurice Sendak.
Bodley Head and Picture Puffin.

The White crane, by Junko
Morimoto.
Collins.

Who sank the boat, by Pamela
Allen.
Hamilton and Picture Puffin.

Who's in Rabbit's house, by
Verna Aardema.
Bodley Head. Available, with
tape if required, from Weston
Woods.

*Why mosquitoes buzz in
peoples' ears,* by Verna
Aardeema.
Dial Books (NY). Available,
with tape if required, from
Weston Woods.

'Wide Range' Readers;
Oliver & Boyd.

Witches four; by Marc Brown.
Hamilton.

Wolf and the Seven kids; by
Brothers Grimm.
Ladybird and other versions

Teachers' books referred to in the text

Alam, Rehana: *Partners in
reading and story-telling* in
Shared reading, shared writing.
CLPE. 1990.

Barnes, Douglas: *From
communication to curriculum.*
Penguin, 1976.

Barrs,Myra; Ellis,Sue;
Hester,Hilary; Thomas,Anne:
*The Primary Language Record:
handbook for teachers.*
CLPE/ILEA, 1988.

Bartlett,E; and Scribner,S: *Text
and context: referential
organization in children's
narratives* in *Writing: the nature,
development and teaching of
written communication.* ed. by
M. Whiteman. Vol.1. Hillsdale
NJ: Lawrence Erlbaum, 1981.

Bazalgette, Cary: editor;
Primary media education.
British Film Institute, 1989.

Bennett, Jill: *Learning to read
with picture books.* 4th edn.
Thimble Press, 1991.

Bettelheim, Bruno: *On learning
to read: the child's fascination
with meaning.* Thames &
Hudson, 1982.

Bettelheim, Bruno: *The Uses of
enchantment: meaning and
importance of fairy tales.* New
edn. Penguin, 1991.

Baghban, Marcia: *Our daughter
learns to read and write.*
Newark, Delaware: International
Reading Association, 1984.

Bissex, Glenda L.: *Gnys at wrk:
a child learns to write and read.*
Harvard University Press, 1980.

*The Books for Keeps guides to
childrens books for a multicultural society*
1: 0-7. 2: 8-12:. Books for
Keeps, 1985-6.

Bryant, Peter and Bradley,
Lynette: *Children's reading
problems.* Blackwell, 1985.

Bussis, Anne; Chittenden,
Edward; Amarel, Marianne;
Klausner, Edith: *Inquiry into
meaning: an investigation of
learning to read.* Hillsdale, NJ:
Erlbaum, 1985.

Butler, Dorothy: *Babies need
books.* 2nd rev.edn. Penguin,
1988.

Read Read Read: 2nd rev.edn.
CLPE, 1984.
Centre for Language in Primary
Education: Shared reading,
shared writing: CLPE, 1990.

Chambers, Aidan: *The Reading
environment: how adults help
children enjoy books.* Thimble
Press, 1991.

Chukovsky, Kornei: *From two to
five.* University of California
Press, 1971.

Clark, Margaret: *Young fluent
readers.* Heinemann
Educational, 1976.

Crago, Margaret and Hugh:
Prelude to literacy. Illinois
University Press, 1983.

Davies, Maire Messenger:
Television is good for your kids.
Hilary Shipman, 1989.

Department of Education and
Science: *English for ages 5 to 16*
(The Cox Report) November,
1988.

Department of Education and
Science: *A Language for life.*
(The Bullock Report). HMSO,
1975.

Dombey, Henrietta: *Learning the
language of books* in M.Meek
(ed.) *Opening moves.* Bedford
Way Paper No.17. University of
London Institute of Education,
1984.

English and Media Centre: *The
English curriculum: media.* Key
Stage 3, years 7-9., 1991.

Ferreiro, Emilia and Teberosky,
Anne: *Literacy before schooling.*
Portsmouth, N.H.: Heinemann
Educational, 1982.

Fox, Carol: *Talking like a book:
young children's oral
monologues* in M.Meek (ed.)
Opening moves. Bedford Way
Papers No.17. University of
London Institute of Education,
1984.

Goelman, Hillel;
Oberg,Antoinette; Smith, Frank:
editors *Awakening to literacy.*
Portsmouth, N.H. : Heinemann
Educational, 1984.

Goodman, Yetta: *Kidwatching:
observing children in the
classroom* in *Observing the
language learner* edited by
Angela Jaggar and M. Trika
Smith-Burke. Newark,
Delaware: IRA/NCTE, 1985.

Graham, Judith: *Pictures on the
page.* NATE, 1990.

Griffiths, Alex and Hamilton,
Dorothy: *Parent, teacher, child:
working together in children's
learning.* Methuen, 1984.

Halliday, M.A.K.: *Language as
social semiotic: the social
interpretation of language and
meaning.* E.Arnold, 1979.

Halliday, M.A.K.: *Learning how
to mean: explorations in the
development of language.*
E.Arnold, 1975.

Hardy, Barbara: *Towards a
poetics of fiction: an approach
through narrative.* in M.Meek,
A.Warlow, Griselda Barton: *The
Cool Web: the pattern of children's
reading.* Bodley Head, 1977.

Harste, Jerome C.; Woodward, Virginia A.; Burke, Carolyn.L: *Language stories and literacy lessons.* Portsmouth N.H: Heinemann Educational, 1984.

Heath, Shirley Brice: *Ways with words: language, life and work in communities and classrooms.* Cambridge University Press, 1983.

Hodgeon, Julia: *Taking a look at the page* in *Language Matters. Reading.* 1990/91. No.3.

Hodgeon, Julia: *A Women's world? a report on a project in Cleveland nurseries on sex differentiation in the early years.* Cleveland Education Authority. n.d.

Holdaway, Don: *The Foundations of literacy.* Ashton Scholastic, 1979.

Huey, Edmund Burke: *The psychology and pedagogy of reading.* M.I.T. Press, 1908.

Hynds, Jeff: *Recent developments in reading and their implications for school and classroom practice.* Avery Hill College, 1984.

Inner London Education Authority: Research and Statistics Branch. *Pupil achievement in reading* (1986) Unpublished.
Pupil achievement in reading RS1182/88. April, 1988.
Reading experience of pupils: validation survey of reading. Scale 2 from the Primary Language Record. RS 1285/90. March, 1990.

Jackson,A; and Hannon,P: *The Belfield reading project.* Rochdale: Belfield Community Council, 1981.

Johnson,Paul: *A Book of one's own: developing literacy through making books.* Hodder & Stoughton, 1991.

Language Matters: Information books. 1990/91. No.2.

Language Matters: Story and Storytelling. 1988. No.2/3.

Lutrario, Chris: editor *Hooked on books.* Harcourt, Brace, Jovanovich, 1991. Video obtainable from Educational Media International.

Meek, Margaret: *How texts teach what readers learn.* Thimble Press, 1988.

Meek, Margaret; *Learning to read.* Bodley Head, 1986.

Meek, Margaret: *On being literate: living with difference.* Bodley Head, 1990.

Minns, Hilary: *Primary language: extending the curriculum with computers.* NCET, 1991.

Minns, Hilary: *Read it to me now!: learning at home and at school.* Virago, 1990.

Moon, Cliff: *Individualised reading.* Reading and Language Information Centre. Reading, Berkshire.

Moss, Elaine: *What is a 'good' book?: the 'Peppermint' lesson* in *The Cool Web: the pattern of children's reading* ed. by M.Meek, A.Warlow, G.Barton. Bodley Head, 1977.

The National Writing Project: *Writing partnerships 1 and 2.* Nelson, 1990.

Neisser, Ulrich: *Cognitive psychology.* New York: Appleton-Century-Crofts, 1967.

Osmont, Pip: G*irls, boys and reading* in *Stop, look and listen: an account of girls' and boys' achievement in reading and mathematics in the primary school.* ILEA, 1987.

Payton, Shirley: *Developing awareness of print: young child's first steps towards literacy.* Education Review, University of Birmingham, 1984.

Phinney, Margaret Yatsevitch: *Reading with the troubled reader.* Scholastic, 1988.

Pidgeon, Sue: *Helping your child with reading and writing.* Puffin Book Club,. n.d.

Rieser, Richard; and Mason, Micheline: *Disability equality in the classroom: a human rights issue.* ILEA, 1990. Now available from the author at Hackney Professional Development Centre, Albion Drive, London, E8 4ET.

Roll, David: *What language shall we talk today: an exploration of children's home literacy contexts and bilingualism.* Unpublished study, Avery Hill College. Advanced Diploma in Reading and Writing, 1988. Copy held by CLPE.

Rumelhart,David E.: *Toward an interactive model of reading* in S.Dornic (ed) *Attention and performance VI : proceedings of the 6th International Symposium on Attention and Performance, Stockholm, Sweden, 1975.* Halsted Press, 1977.

Schieffelin, Bambi and Gilmore, Perry (eds) : *The Acquisition of literacy: ethnographic perspectives.* Norwood, N.J.: Ablex, 1986.

School libraries: *steps in the right direction. Guidelines for a school library resource centre.* School Library Association, 1989.

Tizard, J.; Schofield, W.; and Hewison, J: *Collaboration between teachers and parents in assisting children's reading* in *British Journal of Educational Psychology*, Vol.52. 1982. p1-15.

Torrey, Janes: *Learning to read without a teacher: a case study* in *Psycholinguistics and reading*; edited by Frank Smith. N.Y. Holt, Rinehart and Winston, 1973.

Trelease, Jim: *The Read-aloud handbook.* Penguin, 1982.

Vellender, Anne: *Teacher inquiry in the classroom: what's in a name? Literacy events in an infant classroom* in *Language Arts* Vol.66 No.5. September, 1989 (see also Anne Washtell)

Vygotsky, Lev: *Mind in society: the development of higher psychological processes.* Harvard University Press, 1978.

Washtell, Anne: *Names and Nominations: Literacy events in an Infant classroom.* University of London Institute of Education. Unpublished M.A. Dissertation, 1989.

Waterland, Liz: *Read with me: an apprenticeship approach to reading.* Rev. 2nd edn. Thimble Press, 1988.

Webster, Alec and McConnell, Christine: *Children with speech and language difficulties.* Cassell, 1987.

Wells, Gordon: *Learning through interaction: the study of language development.* Cambridge University Press, 1981.

Wells, Gordon: *The Meaning makers: children learning language and using language to learn.* Hodder and Stoughton, 1986.

Widlake, Paul and MacLeod, Flora: *Raising standards: parental involvement programmes and the language performance of children: a report.* Coventry: Community Education Development Centre, 1984.

Yard, Lynda: *Communications: developmental learning, reading in the early years.* Education Department, London Borough of Croydon, n.d.

Yard, Lynda: *Monitoring and assessing development* in Wade, Barrie: *Reading for real.* Open University Press, 1990.

Young, Peter, and Tyre, Colin: *Dyslexia or illiteracy?* Open University Press, 1983.

Addresses

Adult Literacy and Basic Skills Unit. 229, High Holborn, London, WC1 7DA.

Books for Keeps, the children's book magazine. 6, Brightfield Road, Lee, London, SE12 8QF

Books for Students. Bird Road, Heathcote, Warwick, CV34 6TB.

Brent Library Information Resources Centre, Brentfield Road, London, NW10 8HE.

Children's Book Foundation. Book Trust, Book House, 45, East Hill, London, SW18 2QZ.

Culture Waves Ltd, P.O.Box 1301, London N16 5YS

Dragon's Teeth. NCRCB, c/o 18, Hertslet Road, London, N7 7JP.

Hackney Schools Publishing Project; Hackney Professional Development Centre, Albion Drive, London, E8 4ET.

Letterbox Library. Unit 2D, Leroy House, 436, Essex Road, London, N1 3QP.

Library for the Handicapped Child. Institute of Education, 20, Bedford Way, London, WC1H OAP.

Poetry Library. Education Department, South Bank Centre, Royal Festival Hall, London, SE1 8XX.

The School Librarian. The School Library Association, Liden Library, Barrington Close, Liden, Swindon, SN3 6HF.